The AZCs of Self-Esteem

Dr. Alice Z. Castner

*"Mediocrity is self-inflicted.
Genius is self-bestowed."*
—Walter Russell

The AZCs of Self-Esteem
Copyright © 2003 by Alice Zacharias Castner

Cover photographs © Allen Castner

All rights reserved. No part of this book may be used or reproduced in any manner whatsoever without written permission except in the case of brief quotations embodied in articles and reviews.

Published by

6137 East Mescal Street
Scottsdale, AZ 85254-5418

ISBN: 0-9651835-2-1

Printed by Lightning Source
La Vergne, TN

cover photograph of Leslie Castner Krueger
photograph taken by Allen G. Castner

For my grandchildren

Allen, Morgan, Chelsea, Clayton

Alice, Adam, and Ethan

TABLE OF CONTENTS

PRÉCIS

FOREWORD — *A Personal Statement About Self-Esteem*

CHAPTERS   *Page*

I.	*I Began to Cry* How to nurture one's own growth and development.	1
II.	*Mirror, Mirror on the Wall* Build a positive identity.	10
III.	*I Am My Own Worst Enemy* Eliminate self-defeating behavior.	31
IV.	*I Am What I Own* Be free of possessiveness.	43
V.	*It Is Ever Thus* Grow healthy relationships.	54
VI.	*By the Sweat of Thy Brow* Create satisfying working relationships.	64
VII.	*Getting Back to Basics* Self-esteem is basic to learning how to learn.	74
VIII.	*As Ye Sow* Grow younger with the years.	86
IX.	*Giving Yourself A Hearing* Record and work with the data of one's life.	98
X.	*And So?* Let go.	111

STRATEGIES FOR ENHANCING SELF-ESTEEM   127

AFTERWORD   133

REFERENCES   135

PRÉCIS

I. *I Began to Cry*
The slap on the rear is the classic introduction of most babies to this world. The effects from that moment on of being nurtured and affirmed versus being rejected and demeaned are explored. Many of us impoverish ourselves by giving away extraordinary amounts of power in the quest for affirmation from others, instead of learning how to nurture and esteem ourselves.

II. *Mirror, Mirror on the Wall*
How we esteem ourselves is closely related to our identity formation. Identity begins from the moment of birth and continues throughout life into old age. I discuss how we learn to esteem ourselves positively or negatively at various stages of development. Anecdotes are used to illustrate how we can learn to trust ourselves and our intuition in each of these stages. We need to be flexible; we can learn to look at life realistically with its promise of hope and growth.

III. *I Am My Own Worst Enemy*
We ourselves forge the chains that bind us to many of the situations and problems that we profess to find intolerable. Often we engage in self-defeating behavior so that we won't have to grow and change. That kind of behavior helps produce low self-esteem. I suggest ways to study the self-defeating strategies we use so that we can eliminate them and live more productive lives.

IV. *I Am What I Own*
We often are identified by our possessions and seem to be valued in terms of what it is we possess. "Possessing" is a paradoxical concept. Often we own something only to discover it owns us. I explore also what it means to enter into possessive relationships and how it is that we use/abuse the most priceless possession of all — ourselves.

V. *It Is Ever Thus*
This chapter begins with an anecdote about my newly married daughter who asked me why her husband still wanted to "hang out" with his high school buddies. I told her to resign herself to doing what he wants to do. As I reflected upon this advice, I began to explore more fully my beliefs about love relationships. I address these questions: What does it take to love in a nurturing, wholesome way? How is it possible to have healthy love relationships instead of unhealthy, addictive ones? How can we help others learn to love themselves? I end the chapter with a letter to my daughter with the advice that I wish I had given her — that two people in an intimate relationship need the freedom to become all that each can be.

VI. *By the Sweat of Thy Brow*

Human work is an arena for all kinds of interaction and includes a wide variety of motives and satisfactions. People need more than just a paycheck. Identity and a sense of self-esteem are closely related to the job and working environment. I pose some questions to assist people in assessing the quality of working and thus the quality of their lives. A few of the questions posed are: What do I value about working? What can I do to make my labors more satisfying? How do I feel at work? What contributes to my feeling of being up or down? What kinds of things can I do about it? How does my self-esteem rise or fall as I am working? How can I intervene in that?

VII. *Getting Back to Basics*

Proponents of getting back to the 3 R's seem to be overlooking the need to develop psychologically healthy human beings. How we learn makes all the difference in using productively what we learn. In the process of education we form self-esteem patterns and a sense of self. Students can be taught the academic skills they need to learn in a responsive, nurturing environment. I discuss the importance of a caring relationship between students and teachers and of using journal keeping as a means of effective communication between student and teacher.

VIII. *As Ye Sow*

We prepare for old age all our lives, but we seem to be unaware of the fact that seeds sown in our youth will be harvested in later years. How is it that some people actually seem to grow younger as they grow old? What is "old" and what is "young?" I use anecdotes to describe how many old people have learned to live their lives fully and productively. All of us, hopefully, will be old one day. How can we help ourselves learn to continue living in satisfying ways? What can we do after retirement? As our life expectancies increase, we have larger numbers of old people in our society. We need to learn better ways of utilizing their resources.

IX. *Giving Yourself A Hearing*

I firmly believe it is possible for us all to make better use of our lives. We can change negative, unproductive feelings into positive, productive ones that build high self-esteem. By developing skills in journal writing, we can focus our thinking, state our problems, and seek solutions. We learn to give ourselves concerned, loving, and respectful treatment by recording the drama of our lives.

X. *And So?*

How we esteem ourselves permeates every facet of our lives. We all possess more power than we consciously use to grow and to more fully love and respect ourselves. I include strategies for surfacing awareness of the impasses in our lives, for uncovering our learnings, for making connections between what we are and what we are becoming, and for exploring alternatives available to us to make beneficial changes.

FOREWORD

THIS BOOK IS ABOUT SELF-ESTEEM. It is based upon the observation that we human beings are critics who judge and evaluate all our acts, feelings, beliefs, and behaviors. We give ourselves a report of that judgment in terms of self-esteem. If we approve our actions, we have positive self-esteem. If the critic is disapproving, we have negative self-esteem.

We, of course, are our own harshest critics. It is we ourselves who ultimately prepare the labels of "good" and "bad" with some help along the way from family, friends, enemies, peers, and society at large. Everyone and everything that touches us influence our level and quality of self-esteem. Why it is that some people have positive self-esteem while others have negative self-esteem? Why is it that self-esteem fluctuates — sometimes positive, sometimes negative? How is self-esteem formed anyhow? How can we change our own esteeming patterns? Those are a few of the questions I found intriguing and set out to answer.

It is my belief that the better we know ourselves, the more compassion we will have for ourselves and for all humankind. The awesomeness of the human spirit, our capacity for loving and caring and appreciating the beauty in the world around us is something we seem to ignore or take for granted. Often, instead, we focus upon our capacity for hating, distrusting, and seeing all that is ugly. How easily we fall into the habit of seeing what's wrong with the world instead of what's right!

An example of a negative versus a positive attitude: some teachers and their young students in a slum area were once asked to write about what they saw and experienced in their travels to school each day. The teachers wrote about the dirty streets, the bad odors, the grit that blew into their eyes. The children wrote about the blue sky, the sound of the bells on the horse of the junk-man, the color of pigeons. One could hardly believe they wrote about the same place! We are born with infinite curiosity and wonderment; many of us seem to lose those qualities along the way.

I have long been intrigued with the concept of self-esteem — long before I became aware that I had a real problem in esteeming myself. I was the oldest girl in a family of six born shortly before the depression. My parents were German immigrants with a marginal education. They were hard working people who moved from New York City to a farm when I was six years old. The superior status of the male was a fact taken for granted in the rigid

German culture in which I was reared. I learned early, as did my sisters, that our role was to serve the males in our family. This was the beginning, I suppose, of the feeling that there was something wrong with me, that being born female defined me as an inferior human being. Added to this was the fact that we spoke German at home and, although I could speak English, I used many German expressions that made me appear strange to my classmates when I started school. I was the only one who wore brown ribbed stockings pulled over long underwear. Try as I might, the result was always a wrinkled, lumpy mess. My lunch box contained hearty pumpernickel sandwiches as compared to the white bread, peanut butter and jelly I longingly watched the other children consume. There was no use in complaining to my mother; the refrain was, "I don't care what the other kids do, you do what this family does."

It was only when I became an adult that I realized how nutritionally sound and wholesome our food was. My mother was a gourmet cook, actually; but I didn't realize it until the first time I had crepes and became aware that they were the "egg" pancakes we loved and had enjoyed so frequently on the farm.

Although my mother advocated waiting on the male, she did have one belief not commonly held by other family members. "Get an education," she kept telling us. "Learn how to do something." She had come to the United States alone at age sixteen, sponsored by a distant cousin, and became a maid in the home of a doctor. She was never to see any of her immediate family again, as they were lost during World War I. Because she worked so hard, she wanted a better life for all of us. Education, it was clear to her, was the only way to make that possible.

When I was the first daughter of my father's extended family to go to college, I remember my aunt saying, "How is that going to help her? Is she going to learn how to wash the diapers whiter? Let her marry a man who makes a good living so she'll have someone to take care of her."

My career as a classroom teacher began when my husband contracted polio and was unable to work. Our son was three years old at the time. I was fortunate, my family said, that I had something "to fall back on." Although I had been trained as a teacher, I had never taught and had expected to be a housewife for the rest of my life. I continued teaching with short maternity leaves for my other two children and continued my education, receiving my master's degree and doctorate while my children were in school themselves.

The experience of classroom teaching was another encounter with the importance of self-esteem; although I didn't call it that at the time. I became interested in the children who seemed unable to learn to read. One of the techniques I stumbled upon accidentally was the use of puppets and marionette shows for dramatizing stories. I found that many children who "couldn't read" were able to do so when hidden behind a curtain. They lost themselves in the characters, were motivated to learn words, and experienced success. One "non-reader" achieved a three-year growth on a standardized reading test. They were all so proud of their ability to perform, to succeed.

I began to pay serious attention to the study of self-esteem when I had to identify an area of research for my doctoral dissertation at the University of Maryland. My advisor, the late Dr. Frank Milhollan, worked patiently with me, trying to help me find a topic of interest. I remember saying to him, "What difference does it make what I study? I don't care if I study the sex habits of a flea. I want to get finished!" Fortunately, he wouldn't let me settle on just anything for the sake of expediency. I discovered Coopersmith's work with sixth grade students and self-esteem. His study focused upon an area of thinking and research that was to become increasingly important to me.

This book has been a labor of love; it came from the depth of my own living and experience. I have attempted to write in a manner free of psychological jargon and terminology. Often I felt as if I were talking to myself, and I wanted to share what I was saying with you, the reader. I learned a great deal in the writing of this book. I hope that you will find much here that speaks directly to you and that you will learn, as I am learning, more deeply to value and appreciate yourself.

There have been so many people who encouraged and helped with this book. My family lovingly supported me and gave me the courage when the going was hard. My professional family at the Graduate Center for Human Development at Fairleigh Dickinson University gave me resource material, read, and commented upon the finished product. First a student and then a lifelong friend, Florence Pittman Matusky, believed in my work, gave me feedback, typed my manuscript, and found Steven Swerdfeger, a writer, professor, hypnotherapist, and publisher, who also believes in the importance of self-esteem for all human beings.

My thanks to all the students who found my writing to be of value and who took time from their busy lives to respond to my work. I began by teaching them and learned much in that reflective process.

Alice Z. Castner
Scottsdale, Arizona
January 2003

CHAPTER I

I BEGAN TO CRY...

SLAPPED ON THE REAR, I began to cry. Thus began my struggles for self-esteem; the latest evidence is this book. Was that blustery beginning a preview of what was to come? Full of dramatic impact, it served as my ritual entry into the world and now serves again as an apt beginning for this book. I have always wanted to write on the nurturance of self-esteem.

I don't remember my own birth, but it is almost certain that I did enter the world in that time-honored tradition of being held upside down by the ankles and receiving the sharp slap to make me breathe. My mother is no longer alive so I can't check that fact with her. I do know that I was born at 6:30 a.m., that I weighed over nine pounds, and that my father wanted a boy. My father was a German who passionately believed in the natural superiority of the male. The first born child of my parents' marriage, a boy, had died when he was a few months old. And then a year later, along came this female child: me!

Is it possible self-esteem begins at that moment of birth — or perhaps even before? Suppose that during pregnancy the expectant mother is serenely happy about the coming blessed event. She cares for her body, eats healthy nourishing food, takes supplementary vitamins, gets adequate exercise and rest. She daydreams about the child: Will it be a boy or girl? How will it look? Perhaps she even "talks" to her child, telling the unborn of her love and how welcome she will be. Lovingly, she prepares for her coming, fixing a cradle or crib, a nursery, buying clothes. She might even make clothes for the child herself, stitching love into each tiny garment.

On the other hand, suppose a woman becomes pregnant, to her dismay, but she is morally committed to giving birth to the child. She loathes the whole idea, hates seeing her body swell, and grudgingly she will do her duty despite the absence of love.

The environment for the child is being set, although as a fetus she may not know psychologically whether she is loved or not. If she has a mother who values her and loves her, she already has a good chance of learning to value and love herself. If she has a mother who resents and barely tolerates her, her ability to love and value herself is made more difficult.

There are those who believe that the birth process itself is a very significant factor in forming a sense of psychological well-being. Leboyer, a French doctor, delivers babies by a natural birth method, immediately giving the child to the mother to stroke and caress, placing it on her abdomen before the umbilical cord is cut. How different this is from the usual hospital birth where the mother is restrained, sedated, and the baby is pulled and tugged into the world, held upside down, and spanked! No wonder the baby cries — many of us cry from the beginning and cry intermittently for a good portion of our lives.

The kind of response that a child receives as she is growing and developing influences how she feels about herself early in life. How she learns her developmental tasks is as crucially important as learning the tasks themselves.

A child learning to feed herself covers the wall, herself, and everything within reach with food. She hits the mouth target only occasionally. Some mothers during this period patiently encourage the child, praising and assisting her only when necessary. Others simply cannot tolerate the mess and feed the child themselves, spooning in the food quickly and efficiently.

The message received has deep psychological implications. The child who is fed begins to feel incapable of learning to do it herself; she feels dependent upon the mother. The child who is learning to feed herself in a supportive atmosphere is being affirmed in a positive way. Not only is she learning the task, but she also feels the power and joy in learning how to do it herself. She begins to value herself and to trust that she can do it because of her actual experience in doing it.

This how of learning, how we respond and affirm our children's efforts to grow, how we express our love and affection, I call nurturance. The importance in nurturing lies in establishing a balance between too much and too little. Using the example of the child learning to feed herself, we have at one end of the scale the spoon-feeding mother, and at the other end one who does little to assist the child, letting her find her mouth in her own way. Somewhere in the middle is the mother who is supportive, helping the child to grow, yet permitting her to do it herself. She is responding patiently to the child's need to develop increasing independence.

My daughter Lisa has three children; she is a nurturing mother who reads to and tutors them. Now, Alice and Adam read to Ethan. Ethan has benefitted from his older siblings' learnings; he is precocious. When he arrived from New

Jersey for a vacation in Arizona this year, he observed Adam changing his watch so he immediately climbed up on a chair and moved the hands of our wall clock.

As growing and developing human beings, we internalize the attitudes, ideas and behavior expressed by the key people in our lives. We value ourselves as we are affirmed by them. If mother says, "Good Baby" and smiles as the child manages to get some food into her mouth, chances are that the child will smile and feel she is a "good baby!" The child who is constantly scolded and is told she's a mess, begins to feel like a mess; she feels rejected, demeaned. She begins to feel anxious; she devalues herself.

Babies need fondling, loving, stroking. As a seedling soaks up an abundance of water and sunshine in order to grow, so must a child be showered with love and affection in her formative years, or else she may tend to compulsively seek parental love for the rest of her life.

We hear reports of babies in our society who die in institutions simply because they have not received love. No one has rocked them, stroked or caressed them. No one has time to do more than meet their physical needs. These babies seem to withdraw from life, just wither away despite being fed, clothed, and kept warm.

The concept of nurturance is a complex one. It's clear that an abundance of love and affection is needed for nurturance and to help build self-esteem. Too much love, however, aptly called "smother" love, can be as debilitating as not enough love. How is one to know what is too much, what is too little?

In the language of Alcoholics Anonymous, the term enabler means one who, for a variety of reasons, permits the alcoholic to continue on the path of destruction. "I can't put him out of the house when he is down and out" or "I simply can't refuse to give him money; he just needs to pull himself together." An enabler sees herself or himself as being nurturing and supportive. In reality, enablers assist the victim to continue to live in a destructive way. The more loving act would be for the enabler not to support the alcoholism, not to tolerate the physical and psychological abuse. In the long run, not accepting the alcoholism would be the most nurturing kind of support one could give.

There is a film called *Three Approaches to Psychotherapy* in which Fritz Perls demonstrates his Gestalt psychotherapy method. Gloria, the demonstration-client, giggles and tells Perls she is afraid of him. He points out to her that frightened people don't smile, that she is merely trying to manipulate him. Gloria says, "You don't like me or you wouldn't talk to me in that way!" Perls replies, "I care about you so much that I will not support you in behavior that keeps you from becoming an independent adult."

Fritz Perls was practicing his kind of nurturance and affirmation. He refused to affirm Gloria in her infantile, manipulative — and as he labeled it — "phony" behavior. Gloria begins to perceive this, although she was initially angry with him. If she were going to work long-term with a therapist, she says she would choose Fritz Perls because he helped her look at behavior she didn't wish to acknowledge in herself. Acceptance of behavior must be discriminating, while acceptance of the person must be unconditional.

Important people in our lives influence how we feel about ourselves. We value ourselves as we are valued, and devalue ourselves as we are rejected, demeaned, or ignored. If a person values herself highly, we might assume that there have been people in her life who have treated her with love, care, and respect. If her opinion of herself is negative, people in her life have probably treated her badly. We carry within us the reflecting mirror of our social experience, no matter how insulated we believe ourselves to be.

The first significant and probably the most important person in our lives is, of course, the mothering one. It is the interaction with that personality that the self-image is initially formed. I taught a seminar called "Modern Woman in Transition." During the first session, I asked students to write about the first woman they remember. Very often they choose their mothers, but occasionally they "remember" an aunt, a grandmother, an older sister, or a next door neighbor. What all these remembrances have in common is really the identification of the mothering one. The stories tell, over and over, of the nurturance received. "My neighbor let me make cakes and cookies at her house. She never complained about the mess." "My aunt took me shopping for school clothes every year." "When I came home from school, my grandmother always had milk and cookies waiting for me." "I always sat on my older sister's bed watching her get dressed to go out. She'd tell me how I'd be beautiful one day, too."

Isn't it interesting that in asking the question, "Who is the first woman you remember in your life?" that the responses are invariably about the quality of love and nurturance received? One woman in her early forties began to cry when reading an anecdote about her grandmother. She had been sent to live with her when she was a year old because her mother was having a difficult pregnancy. She was never permitted to return to the family again. Although she lived down the block from her parents, she was only allowed to sleep at their home on Christmas Eve.

Her story was heart-wrenching. She told of longing to be with her parents and sister. She described the agony of rejection. Now she is married and shares a two-family house with her sister. Although this woman is intelligent, competent, physically lovely, and apparently happily married, her self-esteem is so negative that she cannot accept and believe the evidence of her worthiness. She carries within the early memory of rejection. She still believes there is something wrong with her. Her perception of not being worthy enough to live with her family remains fundamentally unchanged.

Affirmation is an integral component of nurturance. When we begin to have feelings about ourselves early in life, we form certain self images. These images reflect the judgments and perceptions of the particular social and familial settings in which we were reared. They are formed out of the interaction of ourselves with that environment. Harsh or rejecting treatment prevents an individual from accepting self and causes suffering. A negative self-image is affirmed and reinforced by such ill treatment.

Recently I overheard two sisters — one in her eighties and one in her seventies — having a discussion. The older one became angry with the younger one and said, "Well, you were always mother's favorite anyhow!" She had carried that memory with her for over eighty years!

Somewhere in the process of growing up most of us make the transition from exclusive dependence on the mothering one to allowing others to fill that role. We get "mothering" or nurturance or affection from significant others in our lives, from people we love or admire. The amount and quality of concerned, loving, accepting, and respectful treatment an individual has experienced from significant others is crucially important in the development of self-esteem. We seem to learn to value ourselves as we have been valued by others.

We need nurturance and affirmation all our lives. We seek it as a plant seeks the sun. As we grow, we identify numerous key people in our lives. In our early years, perhaps there was a teacher, a scoutmaster, a neighbor, a relative, or a friend from whom we received love and affirmation. In adolescence, peer relationships become important. In early adulthood, we form love relationships, perhaps choosing to marry one special person. During all periods of our lives, all the people who touch our lives are important in the formation of self-esteem. Mostly, they enhanced our esteem feelings; sometimes, though, they deflated them.

We might ask these questions: How do we choose the important people in our lives? Do we reinforce our own images? Perhaps, when we don't esteem ourselves, we seek out people who don't love us, who put us down, or demean us to reinforce an inner image of worthlessness. Perhaps we choose people who tell us over and over that they love us, and our need to hear that makes them crucially important in our lives. In the absence of a strong and realistic self-image, we might choose people to tell us who we are. It is all so complex!

It seems clear that anxiety and self-esteem are closely entwined. Psychologists say that clients coming to them frequently suffer acute feelings of anxiety, helplessness, and unworthiness. Clinical studies reveal that failure to achieve and the existence of conditions that threaten to expose personal inadequacies are among the major contributors to anxiety. Often, high anxiety levels are accompanied by negative self-esteem. The condition of anxiety may be a temporary one, or it may be deep-seated and all-consuming.

Anxiety in relationships can be produced by domination, indifference, isolation, lack of warmth, and admiration. Again, we have the delicate balance between too much or too little. When children are valued and receive love, acceptance, and support, they are able to overcome feelings of inadequacy and inferiority. Too much indulgence results in pampered children who are overly demanding and excessively self-centered; they have an inflated sense of their own worth. This is also true in adult relationships.

Nurturing relationships produce a sense of warmth, respect, and acceptance. Toxic relationships produce psychological illness. In such relationships, we experience acute anxiety, a sense of dependence, a sense of worthlessness. Toxic people criticize, demean, and judge. Nothing is ever right for them; they can never be pleased. I find that I don't like myself in their presence. Toxins can also be generated by smothering, which purports to be love and caring.

It is so difficult not to interfere in loving relationships. The mother who sees her baby taking her first steps often can't bear to see her stumble and fall. If she cries and the mother becomes over-solicitous, her next ventures may be a long time in coming. However, if the mother murmurs words of comfort and encouragement and lets be, the child overcomes her hurt and tries again.

When we love people, we want them to be happy. If they hurt, we want to intervene, to make it all right. We don't want them to suffer.

Growth, however, is often accompanied by some discomfort, some pain, sometimes even suffering. We need to learn to convey the message to loved ones, "I'm here. I care about you. I'll do all I can to assist you in your time of trouble." Letting be, in a supportive, caring way, is a healthy kind of nurturance.

Group or group ideals can also provide nurturance and affirmation. Self-esteem can be enhanced in a group setting. Examples of this are Weight Watchers and Alcoholics Anonymous. Those groups are organized for a specific task to help people break bad habits and to form positive ones. The environment of each group carries mutual respect and understanding. Relationships are developed in a supportive atmosphere. In that respect we might say that AA and WW become significant others, that the group has the nurturing quality of a mothering one.

It is frightening to grow, to learn, and to change. In the process of changing, a part of us dies and a new part is born. When this happens, we are afraid because we know the old self; it is comfortable; perhaps we don't altogether like it, but it is familiar. The new self that we are trying to become is unfamiliar; we are not in touch with it completely; we feel strange and uncomfortable. In a supportive group setting, members are themselves in the process of change and growth. They support one another's efforts to change; they learn to help nurture and affirm the new selves that are emerging.

In such a supportive group, it is possible to try out the new self. We can discuss our fears or report the new insights we've had. Like a child learning to walk, we take a few tentative steps in our new way of being. The support of the group encourages us, for it affirms the new self by respecting, caring. Our self-esteem is elevated when the group accepts us, finds us worthy. We can then accept ourselves more easily.

It is important to have nurturing relationships, to care about people, to have them care about us. It's important to be part of a caring, respecting group. Ultimately, though, we need to rely upon our own inner resources to nurture ourselves, to give ourselves the love and respect we seek from others. I believe it is possible for us to be our own "mothering" one.

An important component of our inner resources has to do with a sense of power and strength. We possess infinitely more power than we either perceive or choose to exercise. Getting in touch with that power and learning to use it constructively is the task. When we begin to pay attention to the choices which we make in our daily lives, we become aware that we give much of our power away. We find ourselves doing many things which we don't really want to do, things which are impoverishing, which drain and deplete us. We permit ourselves to be manipulated by our environment, by our families, by people on the job, or by those we love. And thus, by ourselves! We bring upon ourselves a sense of having no control over our destiny — like a rudderless boat aimlessly adrift, buffeted by the winds of chance and change. In the absence of knowing who we are and what we want in life, we look to others for definition. We give them that kind of power, the power to define us, to mold us as human beings. When we have positive self-esteem, we reclaim our power and control our own destiny.

When I dialogue with myself, when I draw upon my own inner resources, I become my own significant other. Perhaps this is one of the secrets of developing self-esteem: learning to rely upon ourselves, learning to nurture our own growth and potential. When we are despondent and anxious, we consume ourselves, depleting our energy and resources. We infect people who care about us with our anxiety; our needs drain them, so our anxiety becomes contagious. As we learn to cope more effectively with ourselves, our behavior will not be so debilitating and draining for those in our life whom we value. The energy of our relationship can be used effectively and productively.

Again, I don't mean to suggest that we should never discuss problems with loved ones, nor seek comfort from them when we really need it. However, relationships may be diminished or destroyed by frantically clutching at people when we feel overwhelmed by or are drowning in our problems. Then we become dead weights. If our catastrophic behavior is chronic, we force people to escape or avoid being ensnared or pulled down with us.

I have found that keeping a journal — a way of speaking to myself — is helpful in dealing with my own anxieties over everyday problems. In a way, I am my own therapist in such a process. By recording the data of my life and studying it, I can intervene in any recurring negative patterns of behavior and build upon the positive ones.

Often I hear myself saying to a friend who asks how I feel about a situation, "I don't know. I haven't said it to myself yet." Saying something to myself is an extremely important process. In stating the problem, I focus my thinking.

Writing in my journal is a way of speaking to myself. I give myself the advantage of seeking the data and hearing it as I read it over and over while trying to discover what it is I'm saying and doing. I can hear myself as a significant other might and can give myself the loving, respectful treatment that is necessary in building positive self-esteem.

Along with hearing myself is the element of learning to trust myself. I do know more about me than anyone else. I am the world's best authority on me. Most of the time I really do know how I want to live my life, what kind of person I want to be. When I ask myself, "How would you like it to be?" I almost always know the answer.

When I can really hear the answer, and trust it, and when I have the courage to take the risk to do what needs to be done, then I release my inner power, rely upon my own inner resources, and assume control of my life. That is what I mean by becoming my own significant other, learning to trust my deep inner self, to love and respect that self. Such a process does not exclude other relationships; it helps to enhance them. When we love ourselves, we can love others, and they can love us.

Slapped on the rear, I entered the world crying. Since then, I've slowly been learning to nurture my own growth and development. I know from experience that I can learn increasingly to esteem myself. The choices are mine. The power belongs to me. Having entered crying, perhaps I can exit with a smile.

CHAPTER II

MIRROR, MIRROR ON THE WALL...

"WHO AM I?" I ask myself as I stare into the bathroom mirror. The face that looks back at me is my sister — my brother — my mother. I feel a moment of panic, a wave of pain and anxiety. I see an outer shell, feel no connection to the person inside; I seem empty, a vacuum.

"Mother, coffee's ready!" my daughter calls. I am beckoned back to reality. I have been momentarily identified. My face comes into focus and is once more familiar. At that moment, I am mother. My identity also includes being woman, friend, colleague, wife, teacher, employee, housewife, sister, neighbor, and writer. I am each of those women, but the me inside responds differently in each of these roles.

Occasionally I become aware of a me who has nothing to do with any of these identities. I share a sunrise with a loved one; we are connected by the moment and our caring for each other. As we watch the sky change color, I am aware of him, deeply feel his presence. I also feel myself in that moment, strong, rooted, part of the universe. I am connected, yet I am separate. I am joyously aware of myself. This feels like me.

How did I get to be the me that I am? My identity began at the moment of birth, and I began to learn who I was in relationship with my mother. My feelings of esteem for myself were defined by the identity I acquired early in life. That beginning identity was shaped and formed by the way I was treated. I learned from verbal and nonverbal interaction how those around me, particularly my mother, felt about me.

I do not remember my own moment of birth, but I have experienced birth three times as a mother. I really was not very much aware of these birth processes and procedures until my last child was born. I have dim recollections of the first two — memories of heavy sedation, being strapped on a delivery table, bright lights, loud conversations, and then nothing – waking up hours later in a hospital bed. I knew I had given birth but didn't even know if the child was healthy. In each instance, I had to ring for the nurse to ask if it was all right and whether it was a boy or a girl. Then I had to wait until feeding time to see the child. As I waited, I could hear infants crying in the distance;

one was surely mine, and I could do nothing about it. I felt lonely, frightened, anxious, and powerless.

My third child was in a hurry to be born. She came so fast there was no time for anesthesia. I barely made it to the delivery room. Once there, I was strapped on the delivery table, my hands restrained. "There's no time for anesthesia!" said my doctor. "I'm going to have to cut you, and it'll hurt." So there I was, wide-awake, with a tremendous urge to struggle to free myself. The cutting didn't hurt, as promised by the doctor, but I found myself absolutely panicky about having my hands tied. I asked to be untied but was told that I might interfere with the birth process if my hands were free. I only wanted to be free to receive my child. How could this be interfering?

In the meantime, my body was contracting and the birth was happening. It was so easy! I remember thinking, "I've had worse toothaches than this!" The serious pain had been left behind in the labor room. I didn't even know the doctor had cut me until I saw the blood and witnessed the baby's emergence into the world via the mirror at the foot of the delivery table.

She was immediately turned upside down and slapped on the buttocks. She began to cry. I remember the light reflecting from her little blonde head, turning it silver. I felt a bit anxious when I heard her cry; I wanted to reach out for her but my hands were tied, and I remember thinking, "That's not the way it's supposed to be." I was not allowed to interfere. I wanted so badly to soothe her by touching and speaking lovingly.

She was "foot printed" and put on a scale, screaming all the while. It didn't cross my mind to wonder if she felt the cold metal of the scale, if the bright lights and the noise of the delivery room disturbed her. Finally, she was wrapped in a blanket and lay sobbing until her little thumb found its way to her mouth. She began sucking frantically. I wanted to look at her more closely, but the nurse took her away to get her "cleaned up."

At this point the anesthetist arrived, and a mask was clamped over my face. I was sedated so the doctor could sew me up. I didn't see my baby until hours later, after she was bathed, oiled, and who will ever know what else? What had happened to her in those few hours before we really met? Frederick Leboyer, the French obstetrician, believes that "we must behave with the utmost respect toward this instant of birth, this fragile moment." My daughter's entry into the world had not been treated with respect; she wasn't even treated as a person. It was so mechanical, so devoid of caring.

In the process of delivering thousands of babies in the traditional way, Leboyer became increasingly aware of the infant as a person. He was appalled at our insensitivity to the fear and pain of the newborn and began to explode some of the myths we believe to be absolutely true. Though the infant comes from a world of total darkness, she is blinded by the bright lights of the delivery room. Though she is sensitive to sound, her quiet is shattered by loud noises. Though her skin is ultrasensitive, she is wrapped in a dry abrasive cloth. Small wonder that her first sounds are of pain, not joy!

How different is the Leboyer method of delivery! The mother has been thoroughly trained for natural childbirth. She knows what is going to happen, what the doctor will do, what is expected of her, how the baby will respond when it is born.

Most dramatic is the preparation for the moment of birth; it is similar to the opening of a theatrical production. As soon as it seems that the birth will be normal, and the head appears, all the bright lights are turned off, with only one dim one remaining. There is no conversation; if something must be said, it is whispered. There is a feeling of excitement and a sense of drama.

The baby emerges; the head is not touched because it has been subjected to the pressure of the journey through the birth canal. She is immediately placed on the mother's belly where she can hear her heartbeat and feel the warmth of her body. The umbilical cord is not immediately cut, permitting the infant to receive that additional source of oxygen. After a small cry, she begins to breathe. Even if she should stop breathing for a short time, it is not dangerous as she is receiving oxygen from the placenta. The umbilical cord stops pulsating after several minutes. By this time, the baby is naturally able to breathe on her own. She is snuggled in the hollow of her mother's body, and she begins to move and stretch. Now the cord can be cut.

The child remains cradled on the mother's abdomen, and as she stretches and moves she is stroked by her mother's hands. The stroking is reminiscent of the rhythms she experienced in the uterus, but it also helps to get the blood flowing to carry oxygen to the brain. Mother and child can both feel the exhilaration of that first touching, can share their mutual experience of caring.

The baby is not hurried; she is allowed to move at her own pace. When she seems ready, she is gently placed in body temperature water of 98 degrees. She begins to move her head and her limbs. At last her eyes open! Leboyer's photographs clearly show that these newly born infants are calm, not crying with fear, pain, or panic, and that they are enjoying themselves and their movements. When the infant is relaxed, she is taken from the water and placed in a warmed blanket. Her entry into the world begins with a loving, caring touch.

A French study of 120 children, delivered by the Leboyer process, shows them to be relaxed and agreeable, remarkably free of feeding and sleeping problems. They are more alert, better coordinated, and happier. I would hurry to say that in a very elemental way they esteem themselves, that they have a beginning sense of identity.

It is too soon to know what the long-term effect of this process will be; the study was made of children only up to the age of three. It would appear, though, that the psychological scars of the birth trauma must be reduced by such birth procedures. There is an absence of fear and pain. Not only has the infant been treated personally with loving, respectful care, but the mother has been an important part of the process, not merely a half-drugged bystander. Mother and child have shared a naturally beautiful experience and their relationship begins lovingly.

Another dimension has been added since the Leboyer process of birth was first practiced. It is the current practice of permitting fathers to be present and to assist with the birth. My son Allen was present at the birth of all four of his children, giving his wife Erin love and support, sharing in the joy when the infant emerged. One doctor even permitted him to "catch" his first born child.

One of my doctoral students researched the theory that fathers present at birth bonded more with their infants than those fathers who were not present. A medical doctor I know emphasized how urgent he felt it was for fathers to be included in the birthing process, especially when there are birth defects. The hospital where he practices now has birthing suites where the father is able to stay in the room with the mother and child, sleeping on a sofa and participating in the infant's care.

In this way, the identity of the infant begins forming. This first experience, the encounter between the tiny infant and the mother and father, is so very important. An inner image develops within us, which we seem to carry for the rest of our lives. Knowing that we have been loved, valued, and respected somehow develops a strong vital root system that continues to nurture us for a lifetime.

We human beings are somewhat like trees in this respect. I think of a spot in our yard where three pussy willows have grown over the years. I have a passion for the pussy willows with their announcement of spring. I love to cut their branches, mix them with forsythia, and have huge bouquets in early March to remind me that winter is nearly over. But the pussy willow has a very shallow root system and easily topples in ice and wind storms. Sometimes they can be propped up and secured by ropes until the roots take hold again. Three times, though, the willows have not taken hold again and have died. We've managed to take shoots and root them to make new trees, and we've finally learned to place them in a more sheltered spot. The oak tree, though, has remained in the same location for thirty-five years, only losing occasional branches with the various storms. When we try to plant ground cover in the vicinity of the oak trees we discover that the root system is complex and extensive.

So it seems to be with children, too. Some are like the oak tree and sturdily weather all the storms. Others are like the pussy willows and require very special attention to thrive. Unlike trees, though, we can't look at newly born babies and identify which are like oaks and which are like willows. We can, however, give them that special kind of care and love that will help nurture and sustain them all their lives. We remember the quality of that early caring. In her autobiography, *Changing*, Liv Ullman tells the story of Ingmar Bergman's mother. "When she had only a few days to live and was lying with a tube in her nose, she suddenly said to Ingmar, 'My mother never cared for me.' and she cried." Imagine that, an old, old lady who still carried within her that image of an unloved child.

Early in life, as our identities are formed: we learn if and how we are loved, and the seeds are sown for learning to love, value, and esteem ourselves. If we have not been loved, the ache or sense of loss sometimes persists for a lifetime, even though we find other loves.

Society expects that a mother will naturally and inherently love her child. The old cliché, "He has a face that only a mother could love", assumes that mothers love their children no matter what. There is little training or teaching available to prepare one for the important and influential role of mother. We seem to learn about mothering by experiencing it and by doing it. I certainly was ill prepared for my role as mother, except that I was fortunate to have had a very loving one to use as a model. I was concerned with trying to rear children who were healthy and did what they were supposed to do. Although Dr. Spock's first chapter in the *Common Sense Book of Baby and Child Care* was entitled "Trust Yourself," I nonetheless relied heavily upon the good doctor's advice as well as the ready made admonitions from friends and family. I was very concerned that my children learn the proper tasks at the proper time. Words such as identity, self-esteem, nurturance were simply words not in my vocabulary. That my children learn to value themselves as they accomplished those tasks was an idea completely foreign to me. I didn't seem to know how to look inward, to sense my own inner wisdom, to trust the signals and signs, to even have an awareness of them.

The human body has infinite wisdom, wisdom that we trust and take for granted in many instances. For example, for the most part we trust that the fetus will grow normally. We don't try to hurry the development; it grows as its own speed and pace. How does the eye of the fetus know when to become an eye? When does a nose become a nose? Or, a finger become a finger? The body knows when and how this should happen. We don't question the process; we trust that the baby will be born with the correct number of fingers and toes, and births are usually normal. The abnormalities occur at a remarkably low rate, usually when something happens to the mother, such as German measles, which introduces foreign elements into her body, interrupting the development of the fetus. Or, the mother introduces foreign elements into her body, such as drugs or alcohol, which affect normal human development.

We trust the physical development of the unborn child, and the wisdom of the body. Yet, we seem not to trust the psychological wisdom available within ourselves. When my doctor told me to put my first child on a schedule, feeding him every four hours, I didn't question him; I trusted the expert. So, when my baby cried for food after only three hours, I didn't at first respond. He cried for an hour — and I cried, too. By the time the hour was over he often was too exhausted to eat very much. One day I simply couldn't stand my son's cries; I was becoming a nervous wreck, so I listened to my inner voice which said, "Feed the baby!" I fed him and soon he began to regulate himself. He was happier, and I was too. Several years later, when my second child was born, the theory had changed; it was recommended that babies be fed when they "demanded" it. If I had listened to my original intuition, I would have saved both of us hours of grief. But, I didn't trust or believe my own common sense.

Of course, it is not all that simple, and I don't mean to suggest that we should never look for advice from the experts. I do believe, however, that we need to temper that advice, weigh it, experiment with it, and discard it if it isn't fitting. When our inner voice says yes or no, it might be well to respond to it. Many of us have been so conditioned to the contrary that it is difficult even to hear that inner voice. We've learned not to trust ourselves, and to ignore our inner intuitions.

How does it all happen? How do we somehow know what should come next? Why are many of our inner intuitions so similar in the aggregate? How do we get to be the way we are?

In recent years, many researchers have been carefully studying the developmental phases of normal human development. Each one tacks on his or her own set of terms for various obvious characteristics long observed by students of human nature. There are many academic equivalents in adult development to the terrible twos, the terrific threes, the fortunate fours, the fearsome fives with which we are all familiar. However we view the stages of human development, whichever expert you choose, it seems fairly obvious that human beings pass through, in one way or another, a variety of seemingly typical phases that are not necessarily age-related.

Perhaps the most important thing is not to argue, forever splitting hairs about which year marks the exact beginning of the "mid life crisis" for example, or to discuss endlessly which subphase follows which category. Instead, we might better examine how the various passages are managed, and especially what consequences result from how we do it and how we wind up feeling about ourselves as we live through the human life cycle.

For me, the most immediately useful contribution to understanding the developmental phases of human growth was made by Erik Erikson (1963) who described what he saw as the "Eight Stages of Man." His explanation of the ways in which identity is developed is sensible and enlightening. It is helpful in understanding how we become the persons we are. Moreover, we can achieve some insight into the development of self-esteem. In each stage of life, certain "crises" are resolved, either in a healthy or unhealthy way. In the early stages, we learn to trust or mistrust. This doesn't necessarily mean that, if we learn to mistrust in our younger years, the situation is hopeless. There are other opportunities, second chances, where we can again learn to trust. This holds true in each stage of development. The idea of "second chance" psychology is wonderful and hopeful, and that's the way it really is in life.

The introduction of Positive Psychology by Mihaly Csiksentmihalyi and Martin Seligman (2000), whereby psychologists are encouraged to focus upon what's right about people rather than the traditional what's wrong with them, is an approach to human behavior that is, like Erikson's, a positive one toward growth and development. Erikson's stages are discussed below:

1. Basic Trust vs. Basic Mistrust

In the first year of life, the child begins to learn whether he can trust the world. The quality of care that a child receives during this period determines, to a great extent, the degree of trust he places in other people and in himself. The child whose needs are met when they arise and whose discomforts are removed, who is stroked, loved, played with, and talked to, perceives the world as a nice safe place, and experiences people as being trustworthy. When the child is neglected, rejected, or scolded, he learns to view the world with hostility, fear, and suspicion. Thus, a sense of basic mistrust is being formed which he carries throughout all other stages of development. Learning to trust and to mistrust influence the formation of self-esteem. The trusting child begins to value and esteem himself; the mistrusting one senses there is something wrong with him.

Being trusting and trustworthy is not accomplished entirely in the first or any year of life, it continues to be an issue at every stage of development — including yours and mine. Still, our earliest years are especially formative ones and the early lessons learned tend to stay with us for a long time. In later years, considerable unlearning and testing may be required to change or replace those first lessons. Thus, children who have learned early to view the world with fear and misgiving because of neglectful, rejecting home life can learn to feel hopeful and trusting when they encounter individuals who value them. When school hours are but a fraction of a day or a year, some teachers have questioned their ability to make a difference in or to overcome the debilitating effects of home life on such neglected or abused children. Such teachers think it is not productive for children to have loving, concerned care at school when they have to return to brutal, uncaring homes. This kind of reasoning doesn't make sense to me. At the least, children know someone in the whole world cares for them when they experience a teacher's caring and concern. Many adults mention the importance of a particular teacher who became a positive force in their lives.

As a young teacher, I was a participant in a group studying human behavior. We met once a week for two years. Each of us chose a child in our class to study in a deep and intensive way. I learned so much in that process of trying to understand my chosen child, discovering what it was that made her laugh or cry. I began to see the world through her eyes. It was when I saw what she was up against that I began to truly learn the awesomeness of the human spirit. Her home was a cold, uncaring one — but she had a grandmother who cared deeply about her. That nurturance gave Jane the image of caring that enabled her to reach out to younger children in loving ways. Another teacher was studying a young boy whose life seemed at casual glance to be devoid of any kind of physical or psychological warmth. Yet there was a spark within him that was so loving; we wondered from whence it came. One day during a reading lesson the children were talking about being lonely and alone. This little boy spoke up, with eyes shining, and said, "I'm never lonely because Jesus is my friend and I talk to him." After this anecdote was read, we all just sat there with lumps in our throats and tears in our eyes. How fortunate this child was to have found spiritual meaning at such a young age!

2. Autonomy vs. Shame and Doubt

In the second and third years of life comes the emergence of autonomy. Now the child is climbing, opening and closing, dropping, picking up, letting go and holding on, in addition to walking. He wants to do everything himself; he announces loudly, "Let me do it!" There is tremendous pride in his accomplishments, from flushing the toilet, unwrapping a package to getting a spoon to feed himself. The youngster is filled with energy, wants to move, explore, and do several things at once. He seems consumed with the need to try everything in his world. His sense of autonomy is developing.

It is crucially important at this point that the youngster be permitted to do what he is capable of doing in his own time and at his own pace. He perceives that he is able to control his impulses, his muscles, himself; he begins to get in touch with his own autonomy.

Recently, I watched a child of about two in a restaurant, seated between two young, solicitous parents who hovered over him. A glass of milk was brought to him, and the child picked up the glass to drink. Mother said, "No, No" and took the milk away. "I do it!" screamed the child in rage, his little body stiffening and his legs flailing. The mother called for a straw, held the glass for the child to drink. The youngster gave in and obediently drank. In the course of the half an hour, I observed at least ten instances where the parents intervened in opposition to what the child was trying to do for himself. I wondered if this was the pattern at home, or whether they were conscious of the child's public behavior and worried about a spill or a mess. If these parents are as overly solicitous in daily living, doing for the child what he is becoming capable of doing for himself, a sense of shame and doubt will be reinforced in the child. I saw him giving up at breakfast. He wanted so to do it himself.

This doesn't mean that the child isn't hardy enough to withstand some pushing and hurrying — after all, parents are human also and do have occasional feelings of impatience and annoyance. I'm speaking of the constant nagging and criticism when a child has an accident such as wetting, soiling, spilling, or breaking. When the criticism is harsh and unremitting, the youngster develops a sense of shame and doubt about her own abilities to be in charge of her world and herself. Given such treatment, sensitive children have difficulty in learning to esteem and value themselves.

If a child passes this stage with excessive shame or doubt and with diminished autonomy, she may carry with her accumulating obstacles to make more difficult later attempts to achieve autonomy in adolescence and adulthood. The youngster who moves joyously and buoyantly through this stage is well equipped to be autonomous in later phases of her life cycle. She learns to feel good and right about herself, learns to take risks and to experiment. Her mistakes are not carved in stone; she discovers that making mistakes is a normal part of living.

When we esteem ourselves, we expect that we will make mistakes. We know our moments of doubt will pass. When we learn early that we can be independent individuals who can guide and choose our future, we get in touch with out own power. It is in this important stage that we begin to learn about that power.

3. Initiative vs. Guilt

Now that the child has been firmly convinced that she is a person, she must explore to find out what kind of person she may become. This stage occurs in the fourth and fifth year of life. By this time, she has some mastery over her own body, can ride a tricycle, and can run and initiate all kinds of motor activity. Boys, especially, no longer merely imitate or respond to the actions of other children. The child indulges in many fantasy activities and tries out her language ability, often talking incessantly.

When a sense of initiative has been achieved, the child seems to be more loving, more relaxed, more vital in a new way. She seems "more herself"; she possesses a surplus of energy that permits her to forget many failures quickly and to approach new areas, even if they are dangerous, with joy and with an increased sense of direction.

It is during this stage that a conscience is formed. The child begins to hear the inner voice of self-observation, self-punishment and self-guidance. She is afraid of being "found out." A sense of guilt is forming.

How the parents respond to the child's self-initiated activities will determine whether the child will leave this stage with her sense of initiative far outweighing her sense of guilt. When a child is made to feel that her questions are a nuisance, that her play is silly and stupid, that her motor skills are bad, she may develop a sense of guilt over self-initiated activities that will persist in later stages of life. Children who are given much freedom and opportunity to initiate play activities — making mud pies, tussling, wrestling, running, skating, bike riding, have their sense of initiative reinforced.

Children's initiative is also reinforced when parents answer questions that do not scoff at fantasy or prohibit it. My daughter's invisible companion, called Shimbers for some unknown reason, gave her much companionship at this stage and provided a fantasy world which enriched her life. When I first was introduced to Shimbers I felt a little frightened at what I unknowingly perceived to be abnormal or unhealthy behavior. Since we lived in the country with few children available for play, I became aware that Shimbers served a useful function in Lisa's life.

When this stage has been successfully accomplished, the child begins to feel that "I am what I can imagine I will be." She feels herself to be a worthy human being.

4. Industry vs. Inferiority

During this period from age 8 to 11, the child is more ready to learn quickly and avidly than in any other period of her life. She is eager to share in planning and constructing things. She seems to have an inner urge to make things and to make them as perfectly as she can.

The dominant theme of this period is an interest in how things are made and how they work. There is enthusiasm for minute details. The urge to be productive and the sense of industry is enhanced when the child is encouraged to construct things, to plan, to explore, to make, and to do. When the adults in her world respond to her activity or project in a helpful, constructive way, she is receiving recognition. Being responsive is a way of praising, accepting, affirming behaviorally. Responding in this way is often more powerful than words of praise.

When my son was ten years old, he and his friend Dave decided they'd like to build a hut down in the woods. They found some old sheet metal and pieces of discarded lumber in my husband's workshop. They labored all day long dragging material to the site, hammering, and sawing. We smiled watching them. Had we assigned them the job there would have been complaining and moaning, but the self-designated tasks became all absorbing, and they worked hard without a break. At the end of the day, they smilingly and triumphantly invited us to come look. My husband carefully inspected the job, commented on the nice, tight joints, etc. He had an old door; it just might fit. Would the boys like to have it? Moments later the door was on its way to the hut. The boys completed the hut with a little help from an adult. They were responded to in a way that transcended mere words of praise. They felt proud of their accomplishment.

During school years, a child's world expands dramatically and includes more than the home. Social institutions play a central role in the developmental crisis of the child. The parents are no longer solely responsible for the caretaking role, and whether the child develops a sense of industry or inferiority depends on the actions of other adults as well. This is the period when key people are important in a child's life. Very often these key people are teachers, cheerleaders, and Little League coaches, male and female scoutmasters, or school nurses and custodians. When these adult relationships are nurturing, a sense of esteem is established in the child. Harsh, rejecting comments develop a sense of unworthiness in her. If the treatment she has received at home has been rejecting, her negative self-esteem is reinforced.

When my daughter Leslie was ten years old and in the fifth grade, she adored her young man teacher who had a very keen sense of humor. One day while the class discussed favorite desserts, he said his all time favorite was hot dog pie. "Hot dog pie? What's that?" the kids wanted to know. He described it – graham cracker crust, chocolate pudding, slices of hot dog. It was a joke, of course.

Leslie came home from school and prepared a hot dog pie – working long and lovingly. When she presented it to her teacher the next day, he gallantly ate a piece to the great joy of the class. Leslie had a wonderful year with that teacher, learned a tremendous amount, and she also felt good about herself in that nurturing relationship.

5. Identity vs. Role Confusion

When children reach adolescence, around age 11 to 18, they are faced with the need to establish ego identity. They look fervently for people to have faith in, for causes to believe in and to work for wholeheartedly. This is often a stormy period of life for both the adolescent and the parents. Their bodies are rapidly changing physically; they have many desires, feelings, and sensations that are new and strange. They have periods of acting as adults and then regressing to infantile behavior.

When I reflect upon this stage of development, I have a vivid memory of that female adolescent institution called the "Pajama Party." How I dreaded those nights when young girls got off the school bus at 3:30 carrying their overnight bags! I knew we were in for a non-stop giggling, eating, rowdy, noisy session. The stereo had to be turned up to it loudest volume, no one would go to sleep before 3 or 4 a.m. I tried to be a responsive, understanding mother by providing snacks and favorite foods and chauffeuring to the movies or the roller rink. There always came a time when I said to myself, "Enough is enough!" and so I learned the technique of banging on the wall. This was the signal that I'd like some peace and quiet. The response was always instantaneous. The first time I was driven to wall-banging, I felt a little apprehensive in the morning, thinking I had embarrassed my daughters. I discovered that they were relieved that I had said "Enough!"

Another time I overheard Lisa on the phone saying, "I'd like to go with you, but my Mom won't let me!" I was curious about what I wouldn't let her do and questioned her. "Well, Mom, sometimes the gang wants to do something I don't really want to and if I blame you they don't get mad at me," she said. The reverse of this tactic, "All the other mothers said yes" was also an effective strategy. How happy I am that those adolescent years of my children have passed and that we weathered the passage with a minimum loss of love and respect for each other.

The pajama parties were important, though, because of the sharing of mutual problems and concerns. It was a way of belonging. But it was especially great when my children packed their bags to "sleep over" at someone else's home. It was especially nice when their friends had parents who were also my friends. In this way, an extended family concept developed which was beneficial for all of us.

The point here is that the adolescent needs to find acceptable role models. Often the models are the parents; frequently they include other adults. During this period, the influence of the parent is much more indirect than in the earlier stages of development. If the adolescent reaches this stage with a strong sense of trust, autonomy, initiative, and industry, then the chances of developing a sense of ego identity are greatly enhanced. The reverse is true for the youngster who comes into adolescence with considerable mistrust, shame, doubt, guilt, and inferiority. Role confusion is the negative result in this identity crisis. The youth is unable to attain a sense of personal identity; she doesn't know who she is, where she belongs, or what she believes in. Delinquent young people often exhibit this symptom of role confusion. They seem to seek a negative identity as an alternative to having no identity at all.

The failure to achieve a clear sense of personal identity at adolescence does not doom the individual to perpetual failure. Nor does the attainment of ego identity guarantee that this issue will not arise at another stage. However, if a strong ego identity is attained in adolescence, a firm foundation for positive self-esteem and for a psychologically healthy adulthood has been built.

6. Intimacy vs. Isolation

This stage in the life cycle, the period of courtship and early family life, spans late adolescence to early middle age. During this period, the interpersonal dimension of intimacy is at one end of the extreme; isolation is at the other end. Intimacy here means more than sexual intimacy; it means having the ability to care about another human being and oneself, too, so there is no fear of commitment or of being "taken over" by another. Intimacy includes the ability to have meaningful, mutual relationships. People who have served together under dangerous circumstances, such as, war, hard times, or other hardships, often develop a sense of commitment to one another than exemplifies intimacy in its broadest sense.

I am reminded of a time when I was in a restaurant with a friend. I suddenly noticed that he had tears in his eyes. Without a word, he put down his napkin and went to the door where a line of people had formed waiting to be served. He moved to a young black man, and they embraced wordlessly for a few moments. When my friend returned to our table, he told me that he and the young black man had been arrested while participating in a freedom march in the south during the 1960s. They had share the same jail cell for a few days until they were released. They had experienced fear, pain, and discomfort together while still holding fast to their ideals and beliefs. My friend said that in those few days he learned to know his cellmate more intimately than other people he'd known all his life. "We shared our feelings and values at the gut level," said my friend. "There was no time for phoniness, and it didn't occur to us to play verbal games." They were united in a common cause, and the sense of intimacy was deep and real for both of them.

Another kind of intimacy is the intimacy experienced in marriage. Two elderly long-married friends of mine recently had their six-month check-up. "Our doctor says we are symbiotic," she said to me, with a smile. I felt a little jolt of surprise; the comment obviously pleased and delighted her. The word symbiotic had always had an unpleasant connotation for me; I understood it to be an unhealthy kind of feeding on each other. I questioned my friend. "I think there are two kinds of symbiosis," she said. "The good kind and the bad kind. The good kind happens in a loving relationship when you choose to be with another person. That oneness is exciting and pleasant. You feel an enlarged identity. When you are together, you have lots to tell each other. That's called being in love. The bad kind of symbiosis happens when two people feel an overwhelming obsession to be together. They fuse and can't seem to part. They're oblivious to the outside world, become anxious when they're separated, placing endless, meaningless phone calls to each other. When they come together, all they can talk about is how much they missed one another. Gradually, they begin to use each other up until there is nothing left. But still they can't let go."

This explanation of symbiosis had meaning for my friend and she obviously feels she has the "good kind." This balance of surrendering-retaining self in an intimate relationship is such a delicate one. When you are deeply committed to a relationship, how do you know if you have a good kind of symbiosis or a bad kind? Can the good kind become bad? Is there a critical time when the self suddenly becomes submerged and swallowed up by and involved in a co-dependent relationship? Can it happen gradually? Does it need to happen at all?

It seems to me that the healthiest way to be in love is for both partners to maintain separate meaningful identities and lives. Then the moments apart are not devastating. The loved one is missed and the reunion is joyous. We look at life with delight, storing away anecdotes and reflections to share. We bring a freshness to the reunion, fresh eyes, and non-stop talking about that which we experienced when apart. We seem to become more creative, alive, productive, and able to nourish one another in this good kind of symbiosis.

If we become shut down and barely able to function, when not in the company of the loved one, we miss out on so much. We don't observe the scenery, the drama, and the beauty around us and listen only to that inner nagging, anxious voice which is saying we are separated from our other half. It's as if we've lost a limb, our eyesight, hearing, or a vital part of ourselves. Such a relationship is not healthy or productive. We become unable to engage in our own creative pursuits and, instead, devote more and more time to the maintenance of the relationship. The result is often alienation from ourselves and isolation from our work and our friends.

I have also observed relationships in which only one partner surrenders self completely to the union. The detached partner has so much power in such situations, often becoming manipulative and controlling. Dependency seems to evolve. The attached partner becomes incapable of making the simplest decision and begins to feed off the strength of the controlling one. The relationship may then become toxic and unhealthy, or perhaps the masochistic-sadistic dynamic may be the very element which causes the relationship to thrive. The complexity of our needs and the way we manage to fulfill them through relationships is a fascinating study.

I have experienced both "good" and "bad" kinds of symbiotic relationships in my lifetime; I know that for myself I feel most right and good about me when the relationship is on equal terms. It has taken a long time for me to become aware of this. In relationships where I have surrendered myself completely, I have often felt betrayed, abused, ill-used and have experienced a very low sense of self-esteem. By "surrender," I mean giving myself over totally in an attempt to please another without regard for my own deepest held convictions and values. I lose myself in such a relationship and become a prisoner of it. But when my partner and I won't allow ourselves to get caught up in such behavior, the relationship can become nurturing and affirming for both of us.

Working to maintain an intimate relationship is often difficult but infinitely rewarding. How often I've turned my back on a relationship when I became confused, angry, or simply didn't know how to confront my feelings! Now as I grow older I become increasingly aware how precious friendship is. I know what it is to have loving, caring friends and hope that I will have this for the rest of my life. I don't want to become isolated without anyone to share with, and I realize that caring for my friends and permitting them to care for me is a way to insure the continuation of our relationships.

7. Generativity vs. Stagnation or Self-Absorption

Middle age presents us with the opportunity for either generativity or self-absorption and stagnation. Generativity means we become interested in the larger human family — beyond our immediate family. We are concerned about future generations: the nature and welfare of people, society, and their world. The concept of generativity also includes productivity and creativity.

An example of this stage is perhaps best provided by Eleanor Roosevelt. Her triumphs are legendary: world traveler; eyes, ears, legs, and emissary for her husband, President Franklin Roosevelt. The climax of her life was her work with the United Nations. She thought of future generations, cared about them, worked hard to leave the world a better place than she found it.

As I write this, I find myself thinking that I don't like the word *generativity*. I like the word *productivity* much better. I think this is the real clue in living well at any stage of life; particularly this one. As I observe older people, I become aware that the ones who are productive seem happier, more in tune with themselves and life.

My friend Melba Hobson retired to Florida several years ago at the age of seventy. Melba had been a very successful fashion designer in her own right and had worked with several nationally known clothing manufacturers. Her creations were simple, elegant, and timeless. I still love and wear a ten-year-old black velvet blazer she designed. It came back from the cleaner recently with the label "Designed by Melba Hobson" hanging by a few threads. I took out my sewing basket with the intention of getting a pair of scissors to cut off the label. Instead, I found myself threading a needle and carefully resewing it. It means a lot to me to have her creations; such is the quality of her work.

It had a letter from Melba when she was seventy-seven in which she told me of opening a dress shop called Glad Rags. She loved it, and felt "rejuvenated" (underlined by her). Not only did she feel productive; she had become healthier and more interested in life. How remarkable and how wonderful!

Another older friend wanted to be an artist. At the age of 69, she now has a beautiful, bright studio in her basement. She took courses in printmaking, bought her own press, and is producing lovely art works. She is alive, vital, interesting, and deeply connected to life. She told me that someone had called to interview her for his book on old people. "I was shocked," she said, "I don't think of myself as old." How we feel is, of course, the important point in the aging process. Perhaps we have been programmed by society to feel old. Social security begins at age 62 and 65 so perhaps many of us begin to feel old and unproductive at that time. Since there is a real danger of depleting Social Security funds, we hear talk of extending compulsory retirement to age seventy. Is it possible that we will then learn to become old at seventy instead?

On a trip to Wales, my daughter and I were struggling with our excessive baggage on a public bus. An elderly couple sitting next to us struck up a conversation. They were from Georgia and had been on a month's trip. "This is all the luggage we have," the man said proudly pointing to two bags. "We've learned to travel light, and we're having a wonderful time taking buses all over the British Isles. Cheaper, you know, and we get to see things that can't be seen from the air." No stagnation in these two people either! The thought of learning not to carry excess baggage was a powerful one, and important at any stage of life, but how great to reach old age with a minimum of baggage of worries, cares, and concerns.

People who fail to achieve a sense of generativity or productivity often fall into a stage of stagnation. They feel bored and have a sense of impoverishment. This can happen at any age, I hasten to add, for I have seen a few thirty-year-olds who seem to be stagnating! The elderly seem particularly vulnerable to this condition. Being interested in life and having others interested in us seems to be a way to avoid the terrible death of apathy. If we are more concerned about money or our own needs than others' welfare, we are self-absorbed. If we change what we don't like about the way we're living, we avoid stagnation. Therefore, being old will not be a deterrent to the quality of the life we live, if we have acquired the habit of being responsible for ourselves and to others.

8. Integrity vs. Despair

Through the seven previous stages of development, if assimilated, we reach the psychosocial dimension of integrity. The alternative is despair. A sense of integrity means people can reflect upon their lives without regrets. If, however, they look back and dwell upon what they missed out on, the roads not taken, the blows dealt by fate, or compare themselves to others, despair and bitterness are inevitable. Such people say, "If only I could live my life over, I'd do it differently."

Wisdom and serenity are the features of a well-lived life. It is during this, the twilight stage of life, that many people become deeply spiritual. Is it that death is impending and religion is grasped as a last ditch effort? Or, is it that in retrospect, in the coming of wisdom, one finally sees clearly the magnificence of the universe and the awesomeness of the human spirit? If one also feels a connection to a supreme being, there is less sense of isolation and aloneness. Perhaps, in the belief that there is a God who can love us, accept us, and forgive our transgressions, we can value and esteem ourselves.

The Life Cycle and Self-Esteem

How we esteem ourselves is closely related to our identity formation. We learn early to value ourselves as we are valued; we devalue ourselves as we are rejected or demeaned. How we progress through life also influences how we esteem ourselves. We pass through many identity crises along the way. At each stage of development, we have the opportunity to become increasingly self-reliant, productive, loving human beings or dependent, nonproductive persons incapable of loving or of being loved.

As we pass through these various stages of development, the focus of self-esteem shifts from the outside to the inside. Self-esteem seems to be formed largely in consequence to interactions with others; then, gradually, we become increasingly inner directed, inner intuited, as we become more and more the artists and architects of our own experiences.

I have passed through many of these developmental stages, having reached the stage of generativity vs. stagnation. Life is full and rich for me at this moment. I have important work that I love and that is fulfilling for me. My children have become caring, responsible, and responsive adults; they are my deeply valued friends. I cherish their relationships with me which feel increasingly less like parent and child; although I noted several incidents of role reversals — they becoming like the parent, and I like the child. My son, aware of my asthma attack, quietly arranged to take me to the hospital. Later, I received a Christmas gift of a Caribbean vacation so I could rest in the sun. When I felt depressed, Lisa bought me several bright new lipsticks as a surprise, and Leslie took me shopping. Just a few years ago, I used to do all those things for them, and now they are returning to me gifts of similar caring. I also have loving and caring friends. Life feels good to me.

As I look back upon my life and its various stages, I have an image of an artist at work. I am not an artist, but I have a fascination for the way an artist paints a canvas: brushes a few strokes on the canvas, steps back to study it, adds something — a little more color or a different kind of texture or a tree or...

And so it is with our lives. We all have that wonderful ability to step back and look at ourselves, if only we choose to do it. Just as the artist studies his artwork, deciding what needs to be added or changed, so can we work with the artworks of our lives. We all know those moments when we feel all is right with the world, when we deeply know our essential me-ness. We need to celebrate and affirm those moments — the joy of being in relationship with oneself, of expressing self, of valuing self, of loving self. Then as we learn to love ourselves, it becomes increasingly possible to love others in healthy, mutually beneficial ways.

As I grow older, I see more clearly how pain is importantly related to life. I've always had a very low tolerance for psychological pain, not only for myself but for those I love. I can't stand hurting — in myself and others — and so I invariably rush to stop the pain and to make things all right. But, when I reflect upon the learnings and awarenesses which have had the deepest impact upon me, I discover that often the best insights come from moments of pain. Now I wonder how often I've denied growth in myself and others by making it all right, by not staying with the pain.

It seems that pain has an important lesson to teach us in the stages of life cycle. Without mistrust, it is difficult to learn trust. Without doubt, how can we achieve autonomy? It is the tension between the two extremes which is so important; a balance needs to be struck. The important point to remember is that we always have a second chance or even a seventy-seventh chance. Even now as I write the tomorrow moments are being formed within me. I wonder what it is that wants to happen? I know that if I listen and look, I'll soon learn. I know that listening with my inner ear and looking with my inner eye is so important. As I learn to be open to life's experiences, I find a richness I wouldn't have dreamed possible.

When I ask the question, "Mirror, mirror on the wall, who am I?" I really do know the answer. Not only do I know who I am, I know how I got to be me, from taking tentative peeks at that reflection of mine. I'm moving more and more towards looking closely and appreciatively at myself. I know the directions in which I'd like to move and can almost see the face I'd like reflected back to me today that will be mine in ten years. I need only trust myself, listen to myself, and then have the courage to do what needs to be done today.

CHAPTER III

I AM MY OWN WORST ENEMY

HUMAN BEINGS HAVE WITHIN THEM the urge to grow, to develop their fullest potential, to be healthy, productive, and happy. Yet many of us engage in behavior that results in defeating our avowed values and goals. We ourselves forge the chains that bind us to the situations and problems which we profess to find intolerable.

When I examine the data of my life, I discover that frequently I am my own worst enemy. I am very adept at constructing my own pitfalls and often block the constructive use of my intelligence and energy. Reading and studying my journal show that some of my behavior is clearly self-defeating.

Often I gain insight about myself through observing the behavior of another person. It's as if the drama is unfolding in slow motion on a huge screen before me when an important awareness happens. Recently, when rereading my journal. I discovered a year-old entry; it had little meaning for me at the time it was recorded. As I read this old material, I could hardly believe that I was the author and had missed the obvious connections, which were lying fallow there all the time.

I had recorded an anecdote about my friend Jack who is bright and talented but doesn't quite believe in his own ability. Jack has a mentor many years older whom he respects and admires. This man assisted Jack in getting an advanced degree and in securing an important job. Jack is grateful and loyal to his mentor and has developed a symbiotic relationship that is obvious to everyone but Jack. The entry reads:

> Why can't Jack see that although Fred is caring and supportive, there are times when he is devastatingly cruel? Today Jack was despairing. He had sent his newly written article about meditation to Fred and was happily anticipating the response/reply. 'I worked very hard on this writing. Everyone told me how good it was and I wanted to share it with Fred. I saw it as a way of showing him how much I had learned from our years of association. When Fred's letter came, I was so excited that I could hardly open the envelope. The note was short, told me that my writing was terrible and suggested that I go to Columbia University to study further if I really wanted to become a writer.

I felt waves of anger toward Fred. How could he be so insensitive and cruel? Why couldn't he have given Jack some constructive, helpful criticism? At least, he could've made some supporting comments. Jack says that he will never, ever write again.

I explored with Jack some reasons for Fred's behavior. Fred's monumental ego needs are well-known; he considers himself to be the ultimate authority on meditation. Perhaps Fred viewed Jack's work as an intrusion upon his personal territory. Most important was the question, 'Why had Jack placed himself in the position of having Fred's opinion become so crucially important?'

I felt sad about Jack. He doesn't see how he depletes himself by constantly seeking the platitudes from Fred which are never forthcoming. Over and over, he seeks approval and receives a put down instead of the longed for pat on the head. Rather than basking in the abundant praise Jack receives from others, he chooses, for some reason, to bring about and actually wallow in Fred's rejections. Jack is his own worst enemy!

As I reread that entry a year later, I realized that I was also writing about myself! I, too, had a much loved and respected mentor. I, too, had constantly sought her approval. I, too, had lamented about her rejection of me, of her occasional criticism of my work in progress. Something has happened in this last year, though, and I seem no longer to put myself into that once familiar debilitating position. I seem finally to be learning that we are unable to discuss my work objectively, so I no longer share it with her. Instead, we focus upon other shared areas of our lives — family, friends, and her artwork. Our relationship has changed. It is now stronger because it feels more real. As I have given up my need to put her on a pedestal, it has become more possible for her to become my friend rather than my mentor.

Not only do I not need her mentoring any more, I have become more able to resist becoming a mentor for others. As I gave up the need to avoid owning my own success, I took the power of that ownership from others and gave it back to myself. As a result, I feel stronger and less vulnerable. Now I am more able to assist students in accepting responsibility for ownership of their own competencies.

Why is it that we become involved in nonproductive behavior and give others the power to hurt us? It seems unrelated to intelligence for often the most intelligent and creative people are the most self-defeating. I believe that self-defeating behavior is often related to the ebb and flow of self-esteem.

People with negative self-esteem seem to engage in behavior that reinforces their negative self-image. We create stumbling blocks, through design or default, to prevent the fullest development of our potential. Often we are attuned to the past, hearing the scolding voices of parents' criticizing us for poor marks in school, for lack of competence in sports, for not achieving success in some particular area. The parents may be dead; frequently, though, their voices remain: "What's that 'C' doing on your report card?" "Why aren't you on the football team? I was the star of good old Central High." "Why can't you ever do anything right?"

In later life, the "C" on the report card becomes the boss saying, "Why isn't that report longer? You missed the point!" Although we are adult, the feeling in the face of criticism is the same we experienced as adolescents. When a spouse says, "Why don't you have a better job? Why don't you make more money like my brother does?" We remember the long, long ago aspirations and proddings of our parents.

Having internalized these old negative criticisms, many of us continue to be captives of the past. We've become accustomed to hearing about our failures; we've come to believe that we can't do anything right. Often we engage in behavior that fulfills these prophecies. We become fearful of taking risks, choosing instead to remain in the same old comfortable ruts.

As I look at my friends and acquaintances, I see that many of them engage in various kinds of self-defeating behaviors. I have asked several of them, "How are you your own worst enemy?" and discovered that they were able to identify those behaviors with uncanny accuracy.

One of my friends is overweight, bordering on obesity, with a beautiful face and a sunny disposition. She is very much loved and respected by her friends, extends herself to all of us. "I am fat," she says, "because I don't want to be involved in intimate relationships. It's too painful to become involved, and I'm afraid I'll lose my identity. So I stay fat. Not many men want to get involved with a fat lady." As we talked it became apparent that my friend does indeed wish to become involved. She dreams of marrying and having children, but she is so afraid of rejection that she maintains her bulky size. It seems easier than taking the risk of becoming emotionally involved with another person. She uses her oversized body as a barrier. It's almost as if she's saying, "If you really care about me, it will have to be for who I am inside."

A local garage owner is an example of a person with self-defeating behavior and negative self-esteem. He is a good mechanic, but one never knows if the car will be serviced as promised. Often he breaks appointments, or he just doesn't get around to doing the work after the car has been left for a day. People become furious with him and seek other garages. If he just did the work that came his way, he would be able to maintain a financially comfortable life. Now he relies upon the minimal gasoline business he receives from people passing through town. It's just enough to almost make ends meet.

"I feel as if I have a boulder tied around my neck," says another friend. She does indeed have a boulder tied round her neck – it's her marriage. For twenty years she has been married to an alcoholic who has abused and humiliated her repeatedly. She no longer loves her husband but tolerates the situation. In fact, she seems to get satisfaction from the abuse and humiliation. Her negative image of herself is reinforced. She continues to maintain her negative self-esteem.

Self-defeatists seem to withdraw from experiencing happy and productive lives. They tend to be plagued with feelings of inadequacy and inferiority. No matter how talented, gifted, and attractive they are, they seem to feel inadequate and undesirable, as though it is only a matter of time before they will be found out and everyone will come to the same negative opinion of them. An example of this behavior was the late actress Marilyn Monroe. Beautiful, talented, and revered by the world, she saw herself as inadequate and was unable to find peace and happiness. Self-defeating behavior at its extreme!

When we reflect upon our behavior, many of us seem to have some negative aspects of self that are revealed to be self-defeating. We make many decisions that affect important issues in our lives. I, for example, have great difficulty saving money. I daydream of trips to Greece, Africa, Denmark, or a leisurely vacation in the Caribbean. If I really paid attention to my finances, I would be able to make such trips. Instead, I find myself buying a bathing suit I really don't need plus a cover-up to hide it. I buy expensive books that I could simply borrow from a library for free. Frequently, I buy steaks although I am aware that less expensive cuts of meat have the same nutritional value. When I look at my checkbook, I see evidence of the many decisions I make that simply dissipate my money. I could really make those trips if I paid more attention to my daily spending habits!

Often the decisions we make, influence profoundly the direction our lives are going to take. Many years ago, a young man rejected a college scholarship to stay in the same town with his childhood girlfriend. He told me that he regretted that decision for years. He married the girl and became trapped on his father's farm. He dreamed of becoming a business executive but felt his education was too limited. "I realize I didn't take the scholarship because I was afraid I couldn't make it. It was safer to stay on Dad's farm. After all, I was just a farm boy," he said.

He remained true to his farm boy image for twenty years. When his father died, he moved West and became a truck driver. He tells this story: "As I drove through the desert day after day, making stops at warehouses to pick up loads, I decided I was going to get a job inside where it was cooler. I did. After a few weeks I noticed that the warehouse supervisor did a terrible job; he was disorganized; the place was chaotic. I decided that I could do his job better, and a few months later I got it. After a year, the manager of the plant retired, and they gave the job to me."

At age 44, he has become the business executive he had always longed to be. In the absence of a college degree, he learned the business from the bottom up to the top. He is valued by his company and respected by the workers in the plant who know that he can do any of the jobs there — and will, if he is needed. One of the reasons for his success is the absence of his previous self-defeating behavior. His self-esteem is positive, and he even looks different. While on the farm he weighed about 250 pounds. He has lost 75 pounds of that weight and keeps fit and trim by going to a health spa every week and by climbing mountains on weekends. His life is completely changed.

Examples of self-defeating behaviors are numerous. There are individuals who pretend they are incapable of assuming adult responsibility. They present themselves as poor helpless me and are so adept at it that they get others to take responsibility for them. Thus they rob themselves of valuable experiences which would produce growth and enhance self-esteem. They become dependent human beings, binding themselves to whomever they can seduce into making decisions for them.

An attractive young woman of my acquaintance, Carol, has used this poor me ploy quite successfully, if such power plays can be labeled successes. Although she is quite intelligent, talented, and creative, her self-esteem is negative. When she was accepted into a graduate school, she panicked about whether she could "make it." Her anxiety was real and highly persuasive. Carol became friendly with another graduate student with whom she exchanged ideas. Soon he was writing her term papers, coaching her for exams, outlining the major points of each course so that all she had to do was memorize the lists. He reviewed many books for her and was essentially the ghost-writer of her thesis. Finally, Carol graduated with a degree in social work. It is no surprise that she quickly dropped her so-called mentor or enabler since she no longer needed him, and she didn't want to be reminded of the debt she owed him.

Recently, Carol decided that she wanted to apply for admission to a doctoral program. "I'm afraid to do it;" she said to me, "I haven't written any papers in fourteen years!" The irony of the situation seemed to escape Carol completely. She had a degree from a highly prestigious school, one renowned for its rigorous curriculum, and its high academic standards. Yet she announced to the world she hasn't learned anything. She doesn't feel that she really owns her degree. She didn't earn it.

Carol's self-defeating behavior continues to stunt her growth; she drifts from one mediocre job to another with long periods of unemployment. People who have worked with her complain that she expects them do all the work. The tragedy is the loss of potential. If she had directed the energy she uses in work avoidance tactics toward studying and writing, she would feel that she owned her degree. Her self-esteem would be positive; she would feel more in control of her life.

Some people seem to thrive on being the target of abusive behavior. The man who had been henpecked for years seems to enjoy his situation. "Poor Harry," say his friends, "how does he stand that wife of his?" "Poor Harry" loves the attention he receives from his friends; he contrives in subtle ways to invite his wife's abuse. One of his tactics is asking for permission. "There's a retirement party for John on Friday night," Harry tells his wife. "Do you mind if I go?" Predictably, his wife does mind. He promised to take her out to dinner that night; she bought a new dress for the occasion. She badgers him, tells him how selfish he is, that he doesn't appreciate her, etc. Finally, Harry says he won't go to the party and, yes, he will take his wife out to dinner. "Poor Harry," say the boys, "his wife did it again!" Actually, Harry brought the consequence upon himself by asking for permission. Instead of announcing that he was going to a retirement party, he asked if it were okay to go. He knows how his wife will react; he seems to enjoy giving her the power to decide what he's going to do.

The asking for permission technique is an interesting one. I used to find myself using it when I felt guilty about something. For example, I planned to be away for the weekend and engaged in a group training session. "Do you mind that I won't be here for the weekend?" I once asked my daughter. I knew I felt guilt guilty about leaving her because she had been a bit depressed. Maybe I should go shopping with her or take her to see a play in New York. I thought this but didn't mention it to her. "Of course, I don't mind if you go," said my daughter, who proceeded to tell me of her plans to meet a number of friends for various activities. I felt relieved, but before I went I made sure there were several meals in the freezer, that she had enough money, and I promised myself I'd take her out to lunch the following week, so I went off feeling good about myself.

What have I done when I ask for permission? How is it related to self-defeating behavior? When I ask for permission, I really am abdicating responsibility for myself. Suppose my daughter had said, "Yes, I do mind. I want you to stay home." Then what? I would either have to stay home, missing an opportunity for a good professional experience to which I had been looking forward to for many weeks, or else I'd have to get into an argument with her and leave anyway. I really put the burden of my problem on her. How did she feel about the interchange? I don't know. Maybe she felt resentful, or perhaps she was happy to get the extra money and the promise of a nice lunch, or perhaps she thought nothing of it, being involved with other things.

As I think about that particular weekend, I remember similar experiences recounted by group members. In our initial meeting, I asked the group to write in their journals about how they felt about the weekend, their preparations, their expectations, their feelings during the drive to the meeting place. Many of the wives and mothers wrote that they felt guilty about leaving their families, although they had made the same preparations I had. "I didn't want to sit here worrying about whether they'd have enough to eat," wrote one person. We all laughed at ourselves. As if their families were incapable of preparing meals or even of going out to eat!

Guilt seems to be a critical factor in self-defeating behavior. I am not speaking of the pangs of conscience which serve as warning signals to be heeded. I mean the deep feelings of guilt that paralyze us, prevent us from growing. The kind of guilt that we use as an obstacle to our own becoming: feeling guilty about leaving one's grown family for a weekend is ridiculous. When one caters to that kind of guilt, it is often just an excuse. If I feel guilty, then I won't have to take any risks. If I don't take any risks, I won't have to grow. I can remain dissatisfied with myself and continue to maintain negative self-esteem.

One young woman feels very hostile and bitter about her father. She felt that he never really loved her, that he was always critical of what she did. He eroded her self-esteem by always pointing out what was wrong with the chores she finished. Spots were missed when she scrubbed the floor, silverware had not been polished correctly, weeds were left in the garden, etc. He told her little that was right — always what was wrong.

Her father had high aspirations for this young woman. He wanted her to go to college, to become a teacher. Instead, she chose to take a job as a waitress. "I know I'm being childish," she said, "but I take such pleasure in knowing I've disappointed him. Yet I feel guilty about not doing what would please him. I realize that I'm also punishing myself by not going on to school, but I can't seem to force myself to do it."

Perhaps in time, she'll be able to overcome her self-defeating behavior. Perhaps she'll come to the realization that she enjoys waitressing and will continue to do it because she wants to, not just to punish her father. It's possible she'll become aware that she really does want to go to college, and she'll permit herself to go when it becomes her choice.

Not only do children suffer from the expectations of parents, but some parents feel they have to live up to the expectations of their children. A father, for example, may be fearful that his son will find that he is not perfect. Another father may worry that his daughter's negative self-esteem is related to how she thinks he views her, despite his belief that he gives her affirming feedback. Sometimes it is not what we say, but what we do, our body language, and tone of voice that transmits our true thoughts and feelings. In both cases, the fathers need to open the lines of communication and dialogue about their relationships in a meaningful and honest way.

A powerful emotion and weapon used in self-defeating behavior is anxiety. A little anxiety is a healthy, normal thing. In fact, anxiety or fear serves to get adrenaline into our system, warning us in moments of danger, giving us extra spurts of energy. When we're afraid of the shadow we see behind us — is it a person following? — our heart beats faster, we walk faster, or we run. The signal of impending danger is often useful in mobilizing us into action.

Excessive anxiety serves to paralyze us, prevents us from moving and growing. On numerous occasions, I have experienced anxiety so acute that I literally could not function. I've gone to bed, withdrawn from the world, hid in the closet so-to-speak. Those anxiety spells were often triggered by criticism from an authority figure or by what I perceived as rejection by important people in my life. My need to get a pat on the head was so strong that I would do almost anything to get that longed for approval.

One day I witnessed a friend having a bout with anxiety. She sat beside a swimming pool, paralyzed, her eyes glazed and uncertain, her breathing shallow. I feared she might be having a heart attack. No, I was told, she is experiencing acute anxiety. I wondered what had triggered such a powerful reaction. It seems that, at a party, she had been criticized by her husband. The criticism was so devastating to her that she was unable to function. It was weeks before she was able to come out of the whirlpool of depression, to again become mobile. She spent days in hopeless crying.

This incident had a very profound effect on me, for I recognized the pain she was feeling. I suddenly realized how ridiculous it is to give another human being that kind of power. How self-defeating to be so dependent upon another human being for reassurance, for esteem needs. It was seeing that behavior acted out before me that made me recognize it fully in myself. I didn't like what I saw - the helplessness, the powerlessness, the dependency.

I was determined to do something about my own behavior. I wanted to be more in control of my own life. So, I began to pay close attention to those moments when I felt anxious or depressed. I learned that it helped me to talk about my feelings, sometimes to myself in my journal, sometimes with valued and affirming friends. Instead of going to bed, or "hiding in the closet" I became more active. I went to the movies, to the city, visited a friend, and I wrote in my journal. All this activity helped. It's been a long time since I've experienced severe paralyzing anxiety.

This is not to say that I don't ever experience anxiety, because I do. However, I've learned how to cope with it, how to keep from defeating myself. I try not to become overtired. I continually dialogue with myself about the foolishness, the debilitating results of giving away the control and power that is rightfully mine. I feel much better about myself and esteem myself more highly when I avoid passivity and take responsibility for myself.

Many years ago, I became interested in Karen Horney's book *Self-Analysis*. Her theory made so much sense; I, too, believed that it was possible to be one's own therapist. Then I learned that this book had caused Dr. Horney to be dismissed as a "lightweight" by her professional colleagues, and so I dismissed her theory, believing that one really needed to consult a professional in order to help oneself.

As the humanistic psychology movement gathered steam, I began once again to hear more and more about the inner power human beings possess. We have within us the ability to develop our own fullest potential, said Abraham Maslow and Carl Rogers. It was possible to become a fully functioning person, to become self-actualized. I remembered Karen Horney's theories and reread her writings.

Is it possible that her self-analysis theory posed a threat to her colleagues? They had trained long and hard to become psychiatrists. Now Dr. Horney was saying that people could help themselves, that many of us wouldn't need psychiatric help if we learned to listen and to pay attention to ourselves. Perhaps this is the reason they tried to discredit her. Could it be that a psychiatrist begins to feel that he owns the profession? That he alone can cure us or impart wisdom?

"Do it yourself" kits designed to eliminate the need for lawyers are marketed: How to get a divorce, How to write a will, How to file for bankruptcy, How to form a corporation. Those are just some of the titles. I have not purchased the kits, but it is reported that they are carefully researched and prepared. There are envelopes marked A, B, C, etc. clearly outlining in sequential steps all the procedures necessary for one to be one's own lawyer. Of course, the outcry from the legal profession was immediate. Perhaps there are indeed some dangers and pitfalls, but shouldn't it be possible to file a simple will, a divorce, or whatever? Another way to save money is to find a young lawyer just starting out who may give you legal advice for a nominal fee. Most lawyers believe they own the legal profession.

When we consider the human body, we realize that we know very little about it. In recent years, we've been taught to look for the danger signals of cancer, to be aware of the signs of diabetes. Little has been done to educate us about our own physical processes. Doctors seem to own that knowledge and to guard it jealously.

I'm sorry to say that my profession, teaching, acts as if it owns and controls learning. Only recently have the originators of innovative college programs conceded that we can learn on our own without the benefit of a traditional college classroom. Some schools are giving credit for life experiences only to have accrediting boards question the practice. How do they know, they ask, that learning has taken place without lectures and examinations? Parents are warned not to teach their children to read at home. We teachers own the process; we have been trained; only we know how to do it. Being a teacher myself, I know better!

The point I make is exaggerated to be sure. But, aren't we all authorities on ourselves? Don't we know better than anyone else what we're feeling, how we're feeling? If we can become more skillful at listening to ourselves and working with our feelings and emotions, we'll learn to live more productive, happier lives.

In order to be aware of how it is we engage in self-defeating behavior, is it necessary to understand the theory of the unconscious? Do we have to know why anxiety is caused? Or why we feel guilty? Perhaps it is enough to recognize those feelings of guilt, anxiety, and depression. Perhaps it is more important to work with those feelings to find a way to convert them into positive forces, to become active participants in changing the patterns in our lives.

How to become active in changing these patterns is the central question. How can Jack free himself of the self-defeating behavior that is so toxic and depleting? He has already begun to talk about his feelings to his friends. He is beginning to focus upon the positive aspects of his relationship with Fred, his mentor, rather than upon the negative ones.

I was able to change a pattern of behavior, finally, when I learned the truth about my relationship with my former mentor. I had cast her in the role of the praising and punishing parent. I had perceived her as a valued colleague, one from whom could come feedback and constructive criticism to strengthen my work. As I studied my journal, I realized that, almost always, I had approached her feeling as an inferior seeking to draw upon what I viewed as her superior knowledge. That we were colleagues was a fantasy. I never really permitted myself to be her colleague.

I feel a certain sadness about that. Years and years of perceiving a fantasized relationship, one I never permitted to exist, actually, except in my own head. I've grieved about that but have been able to move on to the new and more realistic realm of friendship, which we both now enjoy. As she recently remarked, "How nice it is to be off the pedestal and for us to be real friends!"

We can't go back in time and undo the injuries we've suffered or inflicted upon others. We can deal with these feelings by becoming aware of them and by grieving about them, if need be. But, then, we must go on living the best way we can. We can learn how and why it is that we are our own worst enemies. We can constructively intervene in our self-defeating behaviors. We can learn to love and esteem ourselves and to take responsibility for our own lives.

CHAPTER IV

I AM WHAT I OWN

"I AM WHAT I OWN" seems to be the American Way. The more possessions we have and the more expensive they are, the more important we appear to be in the eyes of others. We are identified by our possessions and seem to be valued more in terms of what we own than who we are. Worse, we begin to define, value, and esteem ourselves in those same terms. Large bank accounts, homes in a desirable part of town, expensive cars and clothes help make most of us feel good about ourselves.

The owning or possession of things is a paradoxical concept. How often I believe I own something only to discover that in reality it owns me. I have a car that I value because it gives me much freedom to move about. It takes me to work, it takes me shopping, on various pleasure trips, short and long distances. My car gives me a great deal of pleasure and satisfaction. I need my car. I depend upon it for both work and play.

On the other hand, my car is very demanding. I need to pay a lot of attention to it in order for it to function well. I must constantly watch the gauges, fill it with oil, gas, and water; I must check the tires. There is an inspection date I must honor in order to receive a sticker on the windshield attesting to its safety and to avoid tickets. Expensive liability and physical damage insurance may cost annually as much as a car's purchase price. It needs to be vacuumed, washed, and polished regularly so that it looks nice. I feel uncomfortable when it is dirty, satisfied when it is clean and shiny. Occasionally, the car has blemishes (sometimes put there by me in accidents) and has to be in a body shop for an inconvenient period of time. Each season I must remember to have the tires rotated, the fluids changed, and the motor tuned. My car possesses me as much as I possess it!

I have other possessions, such as, a large color television which stands in the living room corner. My husband and son prize it especially for athletic events; the golf matches, for instance, look so much better in color with the contrast of white golf ball against the lush green grass. Phil Michelson's shiny hair and the vibrant colors of the various sports attire add a special quality that is not always apparent on a sun-drenched golf course or on TV. Each season brings its event: baseball in spring and summer, golf and tennis in summer, football in autumn, and basketball and hockey in winter. Each weekend the television seems to schedule the men of my family for some athletic event.

My daughters have little appreciation for sports events, preferring drama, old movies, and rock concerts. A second television set was bought since there was often a conflict of interest in the choice of programs to be viewed. This assures harmony in the family, except that we are divided: the men sit in the living room while the women comfortably settle in the den.

Do we own the TVs or do they own us? Often we are glued to inane programs, mesmerized by the box simply because we're bored and it seems easy to flip the switch. If we didn't have TV, perhaps we'd spend more time reading or doing things more active and productive.

We have become more a nation of watchers than of doers. Rather than participate in sports, we watch them on the tube. Tennis matches, golf, swimming meets, even bowling events are there for us to view. We can enjoy skiing, skating, and running via the TV. We've all become armchair experts in basketball, baseball, and football, shouting to our favorite stars, telling them when they've gone wrong. It's as if by watching we feel that we're doing it too. We become more and more obese, heart disease is increasing alarmingly. We are short of breath. The only parts of our bodies getting sustained exercise are our eyes, ears, and rears.

Statistics released each year indicate an increasing percentage of time spent by both adults and children in watching TV. It seems that TV is rearing the young more than parents, educating them more than teachers. Our children have become more addicted than we. If they are passive now, what will they be like when they become adults?

Over the years, I've noted with interest that whenever power failures occur, letters to the editor will appear in local newspapers and articles will be published in magazines extolling the wonderful discovery of the family. Without television, the family was forced to invent entertainment, games were taken from closets, popcorn poppers were dusted off and filled, fires were built in fireplaces. How wonderful to be able to speak with each other, to listen and to really hear! Sunsets were observed, parks were filled, folks noticed the moon and the stars. How wonderful to be without television! It's as if mankind had been liberated from an addictive narcotic. One would think that we had no control over the machine that it, in fact, switches us on. Nine months after the New York City power failure, statisticians observed an unusually high number of new births. Here is dramatic proof that when deprived of the tube, all manner of creative productions result!

Possessed or possessing? Recently, I read about a socialite who owns a fabulous collection of jewels. So unique and fabulous is the collection that she is afraid to wear her jewels in public. She keeps them in a vault and wears relatively inexpensive replicas of them. When she's photographed wearing her "jewels," it's all make believe. One wonders what pleasure she receives from her collection. Is it the mere ownership that makes her esteem herself more highly? If so, her esteem is outside herself and fluctuates with the value of her possessions.

Do we own human beings? Of course not! One feels an immediate sense of indignation in having wife, children, and friends counted as possessions along with the dog and cat, house, and clothing. "Human beings can't be possessed" was my first thought, but then I realized that I do indeed make references to my children: my son, my daughters. Such a reference connotes ownership.

This idea of ownership is precisely what causes many interpersonal problems. When I own my children, when my sense of identity and self-esteem is dependent upon them, I can't let go of them. They learn to function and to live their lives to please me. When I possess them, they, in reality, possess me. I become so busy helping them live their lives that I am unable to live my own or worse, to permit them to live theirs. When the time comes for them to leave home, if I haven't a life and interests of my own, I might feel a sense of devastation, alienation, and abandonment. And they may also be unprepared, too little experienced in doing for themselves, or in being able to handle freedom.

Many parents manipulate their children in the guise of knowing what's best for them, but in reality they may be seeking fulfillment for themselves. A young man chooses to go to a local state university because he has found an interesting program and a number of his friends will be there. His father is an Ivy League graduate and has always assumed that his son will attend his Alma Mater. He is shocked that his son considers any other alternative and begins the subtle manipulation to get his son to do as he wishes. Because the son loves the father, he gives in and goes to a school he hates. His performance is mediocre; his life feels stagnant to him. But, father is happy and informs the world of his successful son.

A friend of mine has always been devoted to her children. Over the years, she has retreated more and more into her home, rarely seeing friends or engaging in activities other than those of the family. She prided herself in always being there when the children came home from school, in having an immaculate home and dinner on the table promptly at 6:30. Last year, the youngest child went off to college, leaving an empty house and an empty life for my friend. She's devastated and doesn't know how to fill the hours of the day. In the process of being possessive, she became possessed. Her family owns her; she is incapable of functioning without the children to wait on and giving a useful purpose to her life.

I am sure that my friend thinks of herself as a good mother, and, of course, she loves her children and is devoted to them. Wouldn't it have been better for her — and the family – if she'd paid attention to some interests of her own in her life? The inevitable leave — taking of the children would not have been such a traumatic event if she had a part-time job or some hobbies, a creative outlet which she found rewarding. Now her identity is defined by the family, and she values and esteems herself in direct proportion to her ability to serve them.

My friend seems unaware of what has happened to her children as she has served, advised, and possessed them. They worry about her and seem somewhat guilty about being on their own. It's as if she became a boulder in the stream of their lives around which they must flow. If she were able to let go, to really see that the children no longer need her, as they once did, both her life and theirs would be richer, fuller, and freer.

Another friend, Mary, in her late forties has just helped her last child, Gail, leave home. They've had a lot of fun in the process. Gail searched long and hard for a job and finally found one she loves as manager of an indoor tennis club. Mary was there to sympathize, encourage, and listen. She didn't weep and wail about her child leaving home. She rejoiced in Gail's ability to take charge of her own life; she praised the new little apartment and her daughter's decoration techniques. As a result, Gail is free to enjoy her new life; she doesn't feel that she has abandoned her mother; nor does she feel abandoned herself. Both Mary and Gail live their own lives, joyously and productively. Mary is now spending more time on her artwork, pottery, and is building a new kiln.

Intimate relationships, particularly, suffer from the onus of possession. The wife whose identity is totally immersed in her husband becomes excessively possessive of him. She is envious of his job, of his time away from home, and of all the people whose lives touch his. She becomes so obsessed with having to know what he's doing with every minute of his life that she is unable to live her own.

The possessive husband worries about his wife being on her own and out of his sight. What does she do all day? Whom does she see? If she works, what relationships does she have on the job? He uses his energy in an unhealthy, nonproductive way.

My friend told me an anecdote about her daughter, a lovely vivacious young woman who married a man several years her senior. In her younger years, when she entered a room, everyone was aware of her. It was not just her physical beauty that attracted attention, it was that she radiated such joy of life and living. She loved life; she loved people, and she loved herself. She sparkled. One of her outstanding features was long, naturally blonde hair. She cared for it, kept it shining and curled. It was her trademark, and she enjoyed tossing her head as she walked.

Shortly after they were married, her husband insisted that she cut her hair in a very short and unbecoming style. Her long hair made her look too young, he said. Next, he bought her a present: a pair of orthopedic shoes since she was on her feet so much. Gradually he changed her appearance, eroded her self-confidence. She became dowdy and began to have a series of mysterious physical illnesses, diagnosed variously as diabetes, circulation problems, and other ailments. In addition, she became an alcoholic. In her forties, the once lovely woman became hostile, bitter, and divorced. By permitting her husband to possess her, she lost touch with herself and became what he wanted. Because he was possessive and jealous of her, he couldn't allow the world to admire her. He had to keep her all to himself, change her, to serve his own needs, in the guise of meeting hers. During the divorce process, he complained that she was no longer the woman he had married! It is not surprising that her life ended prematurely after a long siege with cancer and long before her mother, my friend, died.

What is the cost of the need to possess or to be possessed? Is it insecurity? The question is very complex and there is obviously no simple answer. If we don't know who we are and have only an identity outside ourselves, we probably don't value ourselves very highly. If we think of ourselves primarily as a mother or just a wife or if we identify ourselves exclusively in terms of work, we organize our life to fulfill that image of self. Then we esteem ourselves according to the amount of service we can perform for our husband, our family, our job, or others. Then we value ourselves according to the accolades we receive for a job well done so we continually seek the pat on the head signifying the approval of others. With an outside-self identity, we feel good about ourselves only when we get others' recognition.

In seeking recognition from others, we abdicate much of the power and control over our own life. Instead of thinking about "what's good for me" and "what I need to do to enhance my life," we use our energy trying to please John, Jane, or whomever. Then we become anxious, for in the absence of immediate feedback we're not sure what it is that will please them. So, we may find ourselves running in circles sometimes, frantically doing this or that in order to hear what a nice person we are, how hard we work, how important we are. We give away much of the power and control over lives when we chronically seek recognition from others. We become dependent. In reality, we are possessed and begin to value self only in the reflection of the outside world's perception of us. We begin to lose touch with ourselves and can barely remember what it is that really pleases us.

Of course, it is not all that simple or clear cut. I'm not suggesting that it is unhealthy to have close relationships, or that we should never do things to please another. I do think it is important to be aware of the effect the abdication of our own power can have upon our lives. As we become increasingly aware of the fact that we are owned by persons, places, or things, we also become more aware of the opportunity to change the situation, by intervening in small but effective ways. We don't have to give up a particular behavior simply because it annoys someone else. We don't have to choose our wearing apparel or hair style to please the people in our lives. Nor must we devote all of our time to catering to the wishes of others.

Several years ago, I worked with some mothers in a New Jersey blue collar community. They were trying to understand their children, trying to become more perceptive of their needs. In the process of closely examining the intimate relationship between mother and child, they became more aware of their own needs and their own behavior. In reading her journal of anecdotal events, one mother made reference to her "afternoon off." "Afternoon off? What's that?" The questions came fast, almost incoherently. "Does your husband let you have an afternoon off?" "Don't you feel guilty?" "How do you get your work done?" "How do the kids feel?" The woman who read sat serenely and said, "Every Wednesday afternoon is my time for myself. I plan what I'm going to do all week – and then I go do it. Sometimes I shop for clothes for myself or just look and try on things if I don't have the money. Or, I go to the movies or pack a picnic lunch and sit in the park and read. Often I go to the library, browse, or just watch people. I never give up my Wednesday unless it's an extreme emergency."

The idea was so revolutionary as to dumbfound the rest of the group. The idea of having some control over one's life, to be able to take an afternoon off was unthinkable. Most of the others were considerably out of touch with their own needs and desires. One week I asked that each group member bring in an object they particularly loved and valued. One woman brought a little religious-type statue that she said she kept hidden away in a bureau drawer. The statue was valuable to her because she prayed to it, asking that it keep her from becoming pregnant! She seemed completely oblivious to the fact that she could have had some control over whether she became pregnant or not.

It was while working with this group of mothers that I became aware of what I called "human addiction." Some of them were as addicted to their families as an alcoholic to liquor or a junkie to drugs. If addiction is the "process of giving oneself up and over," as defined by the dictionary, then many of these women were addicts. They'd completely given themselves up and over to their families and seemed to have little awareness of themselves. Their greatest joys were vicarious ones – through the accomplishments of other family members. Having interests outside the family was unthinkable; attending my particular class was permissible since it focused upon examining the relationship between mother and child. It was something they were doing for their children, they thought, not for themselves. To hear that one could be a good mother and wife, while having some interests not directly connected to the family, was mind boggling to some of these women.

One week we did an at-home exercise in which each woman chose to do something she had never done before — something that was for her alone, for her own amusement and pleasure. Each was asked to keep a record of her feelings about this process, beginning with the choice of activity and ending with the final accomplishment. One woman wrote,

> It took me two days to decide what I could do for myself. I thought about going to the movies or going out to lunch. Finally I decided that what I wanted most in the world was to take a long, private bubble bath with no one banging on the door or using 'the john' while I was in the tub. Once I made the decision, I got carried away with the idea. I made a trip to the corner drugstore and studied all

the bath products available. I finally chose some nice smelling bath salts and added powder and lotion to my purchase.

I went home, floating on a cloud, hugging my secret close to me. The next morning, when the kids had gone to school and my husband was at work, I filled the tub and soaked for about an hour. It was wonderful! I think I'll buy a little pillow to lean my head on for the next time. I feel, though, almost as if I had committed a sin.

The group applauded this small action and gave her tremendous support. For the first time, they seemed to be asking, "Why not do something just for ourselves?"

There is incredible power in the journaling process in a group. When we question ourselves about our motives or when we dialogue with ourselves about situations in our lives, we focus upon ourselves and our own resources. Raising questions that do not ordinarily occur to us is a way of getting in touch with our own power. We open ourselves up to our values, expose our fears, savor our joys. We depend upon ourselves to explore what is happening in our lives. Keeping journals, raising questions, and sharing answers had a powerful impact upon these women. Moreover, they learned to use a tool that would be helpful to them long after the group disbanded.

How sad that the "bubble bath lady" had paid so little attention to her needs and feelings as an individual apart from the family. How fortunate that she was able to identify some small luxury for herself. It was a beginning, a step away from the complete addiction to family. Her ability to begin to view herself as a separate individual made her feel more loving toward the family — she was able to see that she still could be loving, caring, attentive to their needs — while feeling more in possession of herself.

Although I like myself fairly well, I have many moments when I am down on myself. I enjoy my own company, but there are times when I must seek out others or simply get away from the house, the desk, or the task of the moment. One of the things I like to do in those "escape" times, the times of feeling very lonely, is to shop or browse. Among my favorite browsing or shopping places are flea markets, antique shops, or second-hand shops. I love to walk through quickly with a roving eye, waiting to see what speaks to me. I then examine the object, asking myself, "Do I love it? Can I live without it?" Often the answer is "Yes, of course, I can live without it," but sometimes I find a treasure. My treasures include an old weather-beaten tool box – perfect for holding firewood, a pitcher which now holds a lovely arrangement of dried weeds, and an old shawl that I like to wrap around myself when I sit and daydream. I love those particular objects. They are among my favorite possessions.

What is it that I say about myself when I choose an object to possess? The toolbox is probably reminiscent of my childhood days on a farm, but I also love the idea of putting to use in a unique way an object that was intended for another purpose. It's a creative outlet. The pitcher and shawl are also reminders, probably, of something pleasant in the past. I also have a print called "Eve's Tree" which I love. It has my favorite earth colors – soft browns, oranges, and greens. I like the strength and the power of the tree. In certain respects, I see it as an expression of myself. So are the two statues I have, made by an artist friend for me, from the same mold but of different colors. I call them "Mother and Child": one is a soft Williamsburg green and the other is bronze. The green figure is seated upon a graceful piece of driftwood; the bronze one has as its base a piece of Vermont marble. I have long loved these two art works. They are nude, and the woman has an ample but not too ample bottom (possibly like my own) and is seated holding the child. It is the way she holds the child that intrigues me. The child is cradled in her left arm, supported by the mother yet independent and already moving away from her. When I saw this statue, I had to own it. I first bought the green one and then asked my friend John to make the bronze one for my office.

What is it about the statue that fascinates me? Why did I need to own it? I relate to it in a very deep way as a mother. The mother reflected by the statue is the kind of mother I've always wanted to be — one who loves her child, holds it lovingly, yet, freeingly permitting it to be independent of her. Is it an accident that I had to have two similar yet different statues? Now I see that, of course, it isn't. I have two daughters, and a while ago I gave the bronze statue to my older daughter when I went to visit her in the first home of her own. The driftwood Mother and Child went with my second daughter when she established her own home.

Other expressions of self, through possessions, may be perceived through their choices. I have a friend who has a favored treasure of a beautiful bird, probably a seagull; it was carved by an Eskimo from whalebone. The bird's wings are spread, as if he had just touched ground or as if he were ready to soar. There is a tremendous sense of motion and life in that art object. When I study it, I say, "Yes, of course, it is an extension of the way my friend views herself." Another friend, who retired from a very much loved job, purchased a painting that she admired. It is a charcoal drawing of a large empty brown bag framed in a lovely copper frame. It seems to reflect the emptiness that she feels during this particular period of her life. Still another friend bought an old barn in northern New York State; he is converting it into a home. "We wanted to get back to basics," he said. His eyes sparkle when he talks about his reconstruction project. He and his wife will grow their own food and preserve it. A student tells me of her new condominium in a high rise building. "I have to scrimp and save, but it is worth every penny. It's so luxurious, and there are so many young and exciting people living there. I love it," she says.

During the fuel oil crisis in the 1970s, small cars were suddenly in demand. I brought a Datsun and had to wait for its delivery; the demand for the economy car exceeded the supply. I had been driving a Mercury Cougar, a vehicle with a V-8 engine and lots of power. I felt great behind the wheel. What I didn't like was getting only fourteen miles to the gallon. "Why am I driving a big car?" I asked myself. I averaged about 25,000 miles a year because of my job, and my gas bill was formidable. I realized that part of the reason I wanted the Cougar was that it was an expression of my self-esteem. After a series of economy cars, now I have a little car that averages 36 miles to the gallon, and I really enjoy owning it. The money I save on fuel bills is used for other things. In fact, I feel rather virtuous about conserving energy and helping the environment at the same time, and my self-esteem has not suffered because of the change. I don't need a big car to feel good about myself.

For years, the fur coat — particularly mink — was a status symbol for many American women. The ads told us that if we were loved, the man in our life would put a mink coat in our closet. However, if a single girl with a relatively modest income appeared with a mink coat, eyebrows were raised — everyone knew how she got that coat! A few years later, status was indicated by the cloth coat but fur lined. "Not so ostentatious or obvious, my dear," reported the fashion magazines. Currently, young Americans are ecologically conscious and animal rights oriented, so there seems to be an increasing interest in recycled clothing. For a while, old jeans were the "in thing." Now we can purchase new jeans or denim clothing that have been manufactured to look old and worn.

How we dress, the type of clothing we choose, reflects a message of self-esteem. Or does it? My son's business firm sent him to a business training seminar where he learned that he should purchase a gray pin-striped suit to wear to the office. I observed that many businessmen of my acquaintance were, indeed, wearing pin-stripes. Perhaps the clothing we wear is more a reflection of society's expectations of us — or at least our perception of others' expectations. A bearded friend told me he always wears a shirt and tie to the office because people take him more seriously when he appears in that traditional working costume. His favorite outfit and the one he feels more comfortable wearing, though, is an Indian shirt and drawstring pants which he wears only in the privacy of his home.

All of us have articles of clothing that we love, special outfits we feel good wearing. These are the outfits we probably should examine and ask what it is that we like about them. Is it the cut of the garment? Is the line flattering? Or, is the color particularly becoming? Perhaps it is all three. Perhaps the total look feels like me. Perhaps the outfit conveys the message we want to communicate to the world: smart and sophisticated, sultry seductress, sweet peasant, rebel, no nonsense worker, etc. When wearing an outfit that especially pleases us, do we esteem ourselves more highly? I know that I do.

Objects possessed, clothes, things, homes — what is my most priceless possession? Most of the objects in my life can be and are replaced periodically. I have had several different homes during my lifetime. I have purchased and discarded all kinds of clothing, many art objects, furniture, books, and several automobiles. I have learned that I can't own people; nor do I want to do so. I just treasure and value the relationships I have. However, my most priceless possession is myself.

I don't treat my most priceless possession — myself — very well at times. I permit myself to become overweight periodically, necessitating agonizing crash diets. When I don't exercise regularly, a short hike leaves me breathless and blood pounding. Often I give away my power, permitting myself to be manipulated by others. I don't do some of the things I want to do, see a particular play or movie, take a trip to Scandinavia, or simply lie in the sun and relax. However, I am doing some of the things that enrich my life. Writing this book, for instance, is one of them.

The process of accepting responsibility for owning ourselves is also the process of learning to disown those poor substitutes and replaceable objects which we previously associated with esteeming ourselves when we confused mine with me, myself, and I.

CHAPTER V

IT IS EVER THUS....

MY NEWLY MARRIED DAUGHTER was hurt, angry, and resentful. It was her day off from work, and she and her husband had planned to spend it together. He decided, however, to go off with his friend Terry to look at some new diving equipment. "Why is it like that, Mom?" she tearfully asked. "Why does he still want to hang around with his high school buddies?"

I was surprised and a little appalled to hear myself say, laughingly, "It is ever thus! A woman immerses herself in a man; he is the center of her world while she is just an aspect of his. Get used to it, love, you're going to do a lot of waiting and plan shifting."

When later reflecting upon our conversation, I became disquieted. Wasn't I a modern woman in transition? Didn't I believe in separate lives, privacy, and space to grow? Hadn't I given a few lectures urging and advising women to develop interests of their own? "Arrange your lives in order to find time for yourselves!" "Don't let your husband and family be the center of your world," I'd tell my students. "Take the risk of discovering who you are," was my advice to all.

But, to my daughter, I was, in essence, saying, "Yes, it's true that men do as they please. We women must learn to wait for them. It's been like that since the beginning of time. Learn to live with it. Learn to wait."

I felt confused with the dichotomy between the two points of view: one personal and one professional. What is it that I really believe about love and relationships? How do I actually behave in living my own life? Is this an area where once again there is a big difference between what I say and what I do?

"What is love?" I asked myself. What is it that I understand when I speak of love? What is the relationship between love and self-esteem? I became obsessed with trying to find some answers. I turned to my journal and began to explore my thoughts and feelings: I keep feeling that the chapter "It is Ever Thus" is already written somewhere in my head. If I can only quiet myself enough, the words will emerge effortlessly, flowing from head to hand to paper. I'm so sure it's written somewhere within me that I resent sitting down to put pencil to paper. It's time wasted. It's all there on the tip of my tongue, but I stutter with the effort of uncovering it.

I resist this writing because it is too close to me. In a certain way, I don't want to know what it is that I know. Looking at it is too painful, makes me feel centuries old. Besides, I've already lived it. It's always boring for me to retrace the steps that I've already taken. I want to explore other unknown territories, or, if I retrace my steps, I want to at least walk in them in a different way. I'm thinking of the time I walked on a wet, deserted beach, leaving deep, clear footprints. As I returned to my beach blanket I tried to walk in my same steps, but I couldn't do it. My return stride was different; in some places, the steps seemed too close together; in others, they were too far apart. I hated retracing those steps! I became wobbly and could only concentrate on the next footprint. I no longer heard the sound of the ocean or felt the breeze or was aware of the colors of the ocean and sky that I had feasted upon moments before. The game became tedious, not a game.

I don't want to live my life in the same old way. I'd like to walk a fresh path, noting the old footprints in passing but not forcing myself to retrace the steps. I want to be aware of where I've been and the direction in which I'm going, but not at the expense of fully enjoying each day's walking. There is a lesson in the tide, as it occasionally obliterates paths taken, it leaves in its place a fresh expanse of sand to walk in new and fresher ways.

Love and self-esteem — an intriguing topic! Most of the *love literature* I've examined begins with a definition of love. There are as many definitions as there are writers; each one describes what he or she has come to see through particular sets of rose colored glasses. Clark Moustakas, for example, says "to love is to be lonely;" loneliness is a recurring theme in his writings. So, of course, he views many of his experiences through the loneliness lens.

I, too, have a recurring theme in my writing. My inner radar always focuses upon any issue concerned with self-esteem. As a reading teacher, I discovered that children who didn't feel good about themselves couldn't read. My doctoral dissertation examined the relationship between self-esteem and journal keeping. The first course I wrote for myself at the university was "Developing Self-Esteem." I have self-esteem on the brain!

I smile as I reread these beginnings and their contradictions. "I have to live it," I say, on the one hand; and, "I've already lived it," on the other. I look to myself to find, as always, the middle path.

Often, we hear lovers say that a relationship has given them a sense of completion. I think of my friends Susie and Mark. "I found the missing part of myself in him," says Susie. "I feel complete when I'm with her," says Mark. Each experiences the discovery of the "other half" in their relationship. Their love for each other is beautiful and touching to observe. They market together, do laundry together; Susie is present in nearly all the classes Mark teaches. "Aren't they a devoted couple?" the students say in admiration. I'd smile as I watched their obvious pleasure and delight in each other. I also felt a twinge of envy, which I denied and suppressed.

One day an incident occurred which gave me a new perspective about their relationship. Susie came to borrow a pen from me, and we chatted for a few minutes. As we talked, Mark came from their house and started up the hill toward town. Susie immediately ran to the window. "I wonder where he's going?" she voiced anxiously. "Probably to get the paper" was my observation. But, I had lost Susie. "I wonder if he's mad at me for coming over here alone. He's never left the house before without telling me where he was going." Her anxiety mounted; in a few minutes she was in tears, racing up the hill after him. A short time later, I saw them return to their house, hand in hand, chatting animatedly.

In those few minutes, I perceived something in the relationship that seemed amiss. Now the constant togetherness, the unceasing absorption in each other, did not seem quite so beautiful. Was Mark punishing Susie for her little show of independence by coming to my house alone? Why did Susie immediately assume he was "mad" at her? I seemed to have witnessed a little game of manipulation and control, played by both partners.

How good is it for people to be together constantly? What happens to the individual selves? There seems to be a fine line between devoted love and unhealthy addiction. Are these elements present in all relationships but take root only when certain conditions prevail? Why do some people have seemingly healthy love relationships while others engage in debilitating, addictive ones? I think of cancer research suggesting that cancer grows and spreads when the body's immunologic system is neutralized. A *New York Times* article described new information about how the body's normal defenses are avoided by a cancer growth. It appears that certain tumors form cocoons which provide a shield against the body's immune system. Within the cocoons, the tumor is protected so it thrives and grows.

Might not a similar condition exist with some lovers? Do they manufacture cocoons to insulate themselves from the outside world? In an attempt to protect their beautiful relationship, do they also create an environment which permits unhealthy behaviors to flourish and grow, eventually taking them over completely? Are some lovers caught in the debilitating prisons of self-made cocoons, left to feed off one another in an addictive fashion? Or, do some lovers unconsciously seek a state of addiction and mistakenly call it love?

The idea of relating addiction to love seems strange. We tend to perceive addiction in terms of drugs, alcohol, tobacco, and food. Many people are addicted to work, play, shopping, or hobbies. The word addiction carries with it a negative connotation. Love is good, noble, and uplifting. How is it possible to be in love and to be addicted?

When a relationship is all-consuming, when one seeks to fulfill one's own personal needs exclusively through another, a state of addiction exists. The loss of self, the giving of one's soul to another, is that a requirement of love? Obviously not! What happens to our sense of self-worth or self-esteem when we give ourselves completely to another? We become dependent, powerless. We only feel good about ourselves when we receive approval from the one to whom we are in bondage. However, somewhere within ourselves we really know that we have lost our identities. The feeling of anxiety, the need to please, the censoring of words, the suppression of our own needs are all clues to a state of low self-esteem. The task is to intervene when we become aware of what is happening and to do something about it.

Over the years of teaching "Modern Woman in Transition," I have witnessed the struggle of students to discover who they are, to get in touch with their real values. "I began to lose my identity in marriage," a woman student wrote. "His career became all important to me. I created space and time for him to work by doing most of the household chores. His colleagues and friends became my friends. Once when he was off on a business trip for several days, it occurred to me that I didn't really know who I was while he was away. My identity was clear only when he was present. When I recognized this, I decided to do something about it. I noticed a poster in the supermarket describing this course, and my husband gave me permission to enroll."

The group immediately pounced on the last statement — what did she mean, he gave her permission to enroll? She revealed that he said she could take the course if the children had a competent baby sitter, if the evening meal was prepared prior to her departure, and if the homework assignments did not interfere at all with the household chores. It did not occur to her to question the ifs. It did not occur to the husband that he was making unreasonable demands. When he went to graduate school, full time, she automatically assumed all the home chores so he could be free for class and studying. In addition, she typed his papers and did library research for him. Neither saw anything strange about the situation. Both felt they were living out the roles society expected of them. With one exception. The wife began to feel that something was wrong. "My self-esteem was so low I felt that I was in a bottomless pit, struggling to get out," she wrote. "I began to feel days of emptiness, knowing on the outside of me that the day might be beautiful or rainy and stormy but not being able to really comprehend internally."

How is it that we accept such role expectation in our society? The dependence producing relationship for many women is taken for granted. We learn it from our mothers and fathers, pass the tradition on to our own children to be perpetuated for yet another generation.

Once married, many women become immersed in the immediate needs of their families, providing food and comfort, play and rest, transportation and clothes. Seldom do they think of themselves alone. The erosion of personal selfhood begins slowly and continues until something happens to intervene in the process. A small incident occurs, and a woman begins to look more carefully at what it means to be a person with goals of her own. The total commitment to homemaking is no longer enough.

Men, too, can want new goals and a greater sense of personhood. While the wife is locked into the homemaker stereotype, the husband is also imprisoned in the role of family provider. Often he sacrifices his own needs and desires by staying in a job he dislikes in order to provide the financial security for his family. He begins to take fewer risks, his dreams diminish; he settles for less and becomes alienated from that which he longs to be. Often he becomes disquieted, not able to pinpoint what is wrong with his life.

The seeds of resentment are sown, the beginnings of anger and hostility find fertile soil in which to take root when one partner or both become dissatisfied with the quality of life they share together. Such a crisis need not be a catastrophe. It can be a signal that the partners are ready for a new stage of living together — if they can only find the way. If each is willing for the other to grow as a person, they are ready to deepen, broaden, and strengthen what they have to share.

When two people have been together for a long time, they are well aware of the many effective ways to hurt each other. Each knows the other's Achilles heel, the area of vulnerability. You might say that in love relationships each partner possesses the BOMB. People who have a caring and valuing relationship don't push each other's "Destruct" button. They talk, try to work out the problem. Often they take issue with minor things: the children's table manners, the in-laws, the way money is spent. Minor issues cause frustration; they don't devastate. They present an arena for working with deeper problems. Caring couples seem to choose the battlegrounds carefully in order to protect the essence of the other.

Two friends of mine have had a long enduring love relationship. Both are bright and well-educated. Both truly care for the well-being of the other. He, however, has need of a mutually exclusive love relationship. She needs additional relationships. He believes that love means sexual fidelity; she believes that sexual fidelity has nothing to do with her love for him. When he discovers evidence of her sexual involvement with another, he becomes angry and hurt and feels rejected. He feels a deep sense of betrayal and threatens to withdraw from the relationship. She becomes angry and asks, "Why can't you accept me the way I am? Why can't you understand that it has nothing to do with the way I love you?"

He fails to see that his withdrawal threats are manipulative. If he loved her just the way she is, he would be able to accept her behavior. The truth of the matter is that he wants her to be the way he wants her to be, involved only with him. In subtle and often not so subtle ways, he tries to change her. He tries to make her feel guilty about his hurt feelings.

She fails to see that she is just as rejecting and nonaccepting as he is when she demands that he accept her as she is. She wants him to be the way she wants him to be — accepting and open — when, in truth, he feels jealous and possessive. Each wants the other to change. Yet, the relationship seems to endure and deepen. Perhaps it's the awareness and caring for each other that makes them willing to work with the impasse. Their ability to talk, to be transparent, and to be self-disclosing helps them to grow closer, more accepting and understanding of each other.

Perhaps herein lies an answer to a healthy love relationship: the ability to accept and value a person as he or she really is and is becoming. If we can accept and value another person as is, we can then learn to value and accept ourselves as is. Feeling secure within ourselves, there would be no need to make ourselves powerless and defenseless or controlling and threatening.

How am I with those I love? I want them to be happy, content, and free; yet, I want them to be aware of me and appreciative of what I do for them. I give my students much freedom in finding ways to learn; yet, privately, I complain to colleagues, "Some of these students don't even know what I do for them!" I want my children to go out bravely into the world on their own, but then I discover subtle little ways I use to make sure they still need me.

"I love you just the way you are," are the words of a popular song that I like very much. It expresses the way I want to be, but when I look at my behavior I could very well, at times, change the words to "I love you the way I want you to be." I seem to put conditions on the giving of my love. "If you're not the way I want you to be, I'll punish you. I'll withhold my love. Then you'll come around. You'll behave the way I want you to behave." I don't like this negative side of myself. I hate it when I manipulate and control!

I am learning how not to manipulate and control, to be more accepting and less judgmental, to love without placing price tags. Working with my journal helps me to see the ways I use behavior destructive to myself and loved ones. Giving myself a good scolding when I've done something I know is destructive is a way I encounter my undesirable behavior. "Now why did you do that?" I ask myself, after I've made a negative comment to my daughter Lisa about her friend. It doesn't change the situation, only serves for her to become defensive and hurt. As I explore and probe my motives, I discover that I fear Lisa is being controlled and manipulated by her friend. I like myself much better when I can say that to her directly without a blanket put down.

Lisa responds more openly when I am direct, and I know she likes herself better in a more honest interchange. When I am sarcastic and mean, she becomes defensive, then feels guilty for "talking back" to me. I really don't want to tie her to me through feelings of guilt. When we talk honestly, our relationship deepens. I understand her better; she understands my concern and can experience it in a way that is not debilitating to her.

I would like my love for others to be wholesomely productive for them and for me. What does it take to love in a nurturing, wholesome way? Without respect for the loved person, love deteriorates into domination and possessiveness. Respect suggests the ability to see persons as they are, to be aware of their uniqueness and individuality. The loved one must be accepted as is but, more than that, for mere conditional acceptance can indicate a lack of emotional involvement. We must value loved ones for who and what they are and are becoming. To insist that they be other than they can be, at any moment, may cheat them of their trust in themselves, of their independence, of their initiative, and of their self-esteem.

To be supportive of what the loved one is becoming requires trust. In mature love, trust is an essential component of the feeling of the loved one. It takes courage to helpfully let be, not to intervene, not to do it for those we love. Letting go and trusting are difficult for me. I seem to be so frightened of not being needed. Just when I begin to see myself as being able to let go, an incident occurs that shows I still have a lot to learn.

A while ago, I spent a perfect day with my three children in the city. My daughters and I went to visit my son at his new firm on Wall Street. We met his boss and colleagues and heard many affirming comments about Allen and the quality of his work before we left for lunch. The day was cool, dry, and sunny; people on the street seemed full of smiles; I loved being part of it all. We bought tickets for an evening play, had lunch in a quaint Irish pub. It seemed to me that my children were particularly loving and caring with one another and with me. I am so proud of them and the adults they've become. "They really are nice people, the kind I would choose for friends," I thought. My cup runneth over. It was one of these rare days when nothing happened to mar its perfection. A pleasant office visit and lunch, a movie, dinner at a Japanese restaurant where the chef entertained us, and then a musical play we all enjoyed. We shared lots of anecdotal data to store in the treasure boxes of our memories to be taken out and shared over and over in the future.

The next day I found myself deeply depressed. "What is wrong with me?" I kept asking myself. "I've just had a wonderful time with my children. I should be on a real high. I was so happy yesterday, why am I so sad today?" The answer came as I recalled other happy occasions. It's as if there is something within me that doesn't accept joyous moments. I must feel that I really don't deserve happiness; it must be related to feelings of self-esteem. I think this particular happy occasion also reminded me that my children no longer need me as they once did. While I'm happy that they are relatively self-sufficient, I grieve that I can't take care of them as I once did. I also grieve because I've not had someone to take care of me or, at the least, someone to help more in shouldering the financial responsibility of raising a family. After my husband contracted polio and was unable to work, I became the family's breadwinner for many years and, in the process, a supermom. However, he was the precursor Mr. Mom, made my absence from home possible, and supported wholeheartedly my academic work. I could not have achieved what I did without him.

To love productively it is necessary to work on helping love grow. How can we best do this? Perhaps a way to begin would be to assess the quality of the outcome of a relationship. What actually happens when I am with a loved one? Is there a zest for living, an enjoyment of the present moment, or is there a feeling of death and imprisonment? Does the loved one like himself in my presence or does he feel small and demeaned? Does he feel my hand softly in his when he is full of self-doubts or does he hear put-downs that serve to deepen his own negative feelings? Does my love affirm him rather than possess and manipulate him? Do I help him stand on his own two feet? Do I help him become increasingly self-reliant? Most of all, does my love empower him to love himself? Perhaps he can know a dimension of his own personal worth when it is reflected back to him in a mirror of loving and caring.

And, how about me? How do I feel in his presence? Does his love help me to love myself? It would follow, then, that one of the most important things we can do for others is to help them learn to love themselves. I've observed in the people I love that when they feel good about themselves, they seem very alive, open, flexible, receptive, and caring. They are able to live more productive and satisfying lives. They help me to feel good about myself and give me space to grow. However, when they don't love themselves, they become angry, hostile, and give off unhealthy toxins. They behave in controlling and manipulative ways. Then I become anxious, resentful, and often feel imprisoned.

How can I help someone learn to love himself? By showing that I love and value him. By telling him often that I see and appreciate the little things he does to make my life more comfortable.

Helping others to love and value themselves, then, is a way to enrich our own lives. The gift given returns, helping us love ourselves, to love our lives more fully and productively, and so I return to ponder my daughter Leslie's original question, "Why is it like that? Why does he still want to hang around with his high school buddies?" I wish I had answered that question differently. I am her model for womanhood. She looks to me for wisdom. I think of the poem she gave me when she was ten years old. I can't remember the exact words but, in essence, it said, "I want to be like you when I grow up because I think you're pretty terrific."

I want the very best for Leslie, as I do for my other two children. I feel I did her a disservice when I advised her to get used to waiting around and becoming part of her husband. This chapter carries the message I wish I had given her. Last night I wrote this letter to her:

Dear Leslie:
The question you asked was a hard one – 'Why does Keith still want to hang around with his high school buddies'? When you were little and hurt or had a pain, you came to me to have it kissed and made all better. It was a little ritual we both enjoyed, affirming the bond of love between us. Now, as a grown woman, you come to me with your hurt, asking me, in effect, to kiss it and make it better. The question you really asked me was, "Why am I not enough for him? Why does he sometimes need to go his own way separate from me?" As you read this writing, I hope you'll understand more fully why the advice I gave you was wrong. It need not be ever thus. I am learning that two persons in an intimate relationship need the freedom to become all that each can be. Each needs to make new footprints in the sand, their paths sometimes coming closer together, sometimes going apart. When two persons are able to highly esteem their own and each other's differences, they are more able to walk together, each helping the other to grow. It takes real strength to love another "just the way they are" because each one is always becoming more than what was. I guess what I'm trying to say is that two persons each need to be free in order to also come deeply together. Thanks for helping me to explore my own beliefs. I love you.

Mom

Feedback:

I showed this manuscript to Leslie and she said, "I really love your writing, Mom, but would you add something to it? Like, in spite of it all, I'm really very happily married!"
Done!

CHAPTER VI

BY THE SWEAT OF THY BROW

FROM THE BEGINNING OF TIME, it has been human beings' lot in life to work, to earn a living by the sweat of their brows. Since then, people have longed to find psychological satisfaction in their work as well as to receive a healthy paycheck.

"Thank God, it's Friday (TGIF)" or "I have the Monday morning blues" are expressions which reveal the way many of us feel about our jobs. We exist from Monday to Friday rather than really live, looking forward, instead, to the weekend or even to that ultimate weekend, the magic time of retirement. Then we will be free to do all those wonderful things for which we yearn. We'll sleep late in the morning, travel, or garden and maybe do all the things that make up our fantasy of the good life. Somehow, we seem to put off until tomorrow the living of life today, leaving undeveloped the potential of the present. The present remains unopened and not appreciated.

In the meantime, the average person spends a great portion of his working life engaged in some kind of work. Until recent years, most men had to labor from "sun to sun" while a "woman's work is never done." Wresting a living from the environment was a difficult, almost totally absorbing task. As our society began to make use of technology, life was supposed to become a little easier. Exacting a meaningful living from the job still remains no easy task, especially today when work is harder and finding a job is even harder.

Why do people work at all? Why do we invest energy in work to such varying degrees? The obvious answer is that people work to earn money. Yet, there is more to it than meets the eye. Human work is an arena for all kinds of interaction and includes a wide variety of motives and satisfactions.

Going to work gives us something to do, a way to fill our days with worthwhile activity. There is purposefulness to the day, even though the job may be boring and unchallenging. It is a place to go where there are people with whom we may interact. A job may even contribute a sense of identity. Many retired people report that they feel lethargic and listless after having given up their work. They feel they have nothing to do. Their sense of self-esteem is at low ebb. They seem unable to develop substitute activities that are as interesting and meaningful to them. It's as if identity itself was lost along with the job.

Work has always been a way for people to identify themselves; names have historically indicated people's occupations. Shoemaker, Carpenter, and Smith are but a few of the surnames that were handed down through the generations and give testimony to the long ago craft from which a family earned its livelihood. Even today, the relationship between work and identity continues to have significance. When introduced to people, we often ask what they do before we wonder who they are. A first question asked of young children is, "What do you want to be when you grow up?" We don't think this is a strange question to ask a small child. Nor are we surprised to hear the answer. "I want to be an astronaut...a policeman...a teacher...a nurse." As I write this, I smile and remember my grandson Morgan's "graduation" from nursery school. Each child announced the occupation he or she was going to pursue. Little four-year-olds announced, "I'm going to be a cardiologist...an investment banker...an ophthalmologist" and other occupations reflecting their parents' careers. Morgan "brought down the house" when he said he was going to be "A Rock Star!" That was the beginning of his daring to be different and being perceived as a leader.

The problem of identity is a serious one in modern day society. Throughout history, human beings were more clearly aware that they were members of a particular class. They were peasants, warriors, nobles, or commoners. They lived in a familiar place for a lifetime and had a particular set of religious beliefs and practices. There were rituals and initiation ceremonies to mark passages in critical stages of life, from childhood to maturity to old age. Male and female behaviors were clearly defined, and there was minimal confusion of roles. There was little question about who an individual was; each belonged to a family and lived out a specific series of roles, except for families' black sheep.

It seems clear that *identity crises* are a phenomenon which appear with increasing frequency in modern times. The old value systems no longer hold true within an increasingly transitory and complex society and world. Modern living requires adapting to constant and confusing change. Vast numbers of people live in congested urban areas. Individuals and families are required by their jobs to move with increased frequency. Religious beliefs are continually being questioned and often revised. The institution of marriage has changed dramatically with many persons creating new forms of relationships. Labor needs change more rapidly as machines increasingly accomplish the work formerly done by human beings. The whole economy continually shifts upward and demands more and more training and skills just to enter the labor market. The whole modern world is in a constant state of flux.

Still, many of us cling to the old definitions of identity, such as name, religion, sex, race, status, and nationality even though these identifiers no longer carry the force they once did. Few other effective means of establishing identity have been developed, which gives rise to confusion, ambiguity, uncertainty, and, for some, negative self-esteem.

Nevertheless, it is expected that we choose a career-identity very early in life. Choices have to be made when one enters high school; those early choices affect preparation for the work market. The student must declare for college preparatory courses or choose to become proficient in some vocational skill. College students must often indicate a field of specialization during their freshman year, often causing stress and confusion for those who haven't formulated decisive career goals.

A key arena for achieving upward mobility still seems to be the educational process, even though schools continue to mirror the stratifications of the larger society. Children of ethnic and religious groups and social classes that are not highly valued in society tend to receive less education in school. Many of these children are selected and sorted out to become unskilled laborers, based upon stereotyping and biased perceptions; sometimes, though, students choose, by their lack of academic achievement, to drop-out of school or to settle for a hot rod.

Skilled labor is often dependent upon the mastery of high school skills, frequently requiring a high school diploma. Generally the more skilled and prestigious an occupation is, the more formal education attached to it. Such requirements seem to be increasing continually. Once upon a time, companies wanted their young executives to come up through the ranks; now it is expected that they hold advanced degrees from prestigious graduate schools of business administration. Yet, education doesn't automatically guarantee a job. It is reported that many Ph.D.s are pumping gas because they were unable to find jobs that match their qualifications.

The possession of a marketable skill is still a great asset. Individuals with a particular skill can go anywhere, work anywhere, and still feel a definite role and status. The person who can repair automobiles can earn a livelihood in any part of the country. He can be equally at home in the urban areas as in the suburbs or country, as long as there automobiles requiring his attention. A recent perusal of *The New York Times*' Help Wanted section revealed six pages of ads for people possessing varying levels of competency in the computer field. This suggests this is a field of preparation for those wishing to learn marketable skills for application in all areas of the market place.

There are many individuals in our society who have never had the opportunity to learn a particular work skill or to hold a paying job. Social and economic circumstances lock them into generation after generation of poverty. Carl Rowan writes:

> A great part of our welfare problem arises from the fact that we allow too many Americans to approach, even reach adulthood without ever knowing the self-esteem that comes from doing a job well. Even children of well-to-do parents are denied this aspect of development.

Chronically idle people tend to be looked upon as the dregs of society. Work is one of the ways in which people evaluate their personal worth and the worth of others. Thus, it is surprising that so little attention has been paid to work as a factor in self-esteem.

We go to great lengths in our society to insure that individuals who are unable to work do not enjoy themselves at public expense. A person who doesn't work had better have some good reason: handicapped, too old, too young. If a person receives unemployment compensation, he frequently must stand in long lines and encounter demeaning treatment from unemployment bureaus' employees. Some of these people are disdainful of those they interview, making the experience as unpleasant as possible.

Those who cannot work for some reason beyond their personal control tend to perceive unemployment as a disgrace and a disaster. They often feel like second-rate citizens. Their self-esteem suffers.

People in lower status positions frequently have a reduced sense of personal worth. In an interview with Studs Terkel (*Working*, 1974), a washroom attendant reflects:

> I'm not particularly proud of what I'm doing. The shine man and I discuss it quite freely. In my own habitat, I don't go around saying I'm a washroom attendant at the Palmer House. Outside my family

very few people know what I do...you say Palmer House and they automatically assume you're a waiter...This man shining shoes, he's had several offers — he's a very good bootblack — where he could make more money. But he won't take them because the job was too open [public]. He doesn't want to be seen shining shoes.

In our quest for esteem connected with work, terminology seems to assume a great deal of importance. The janitor prefers to be called a custodian; the garbage collector, a sanitary engineer; the gravedigger, a caretaker. With the advent of computers, word processor became a euphemism for typist, which is usually perceived as a woman's job. It's as if the job title makes the service rendered less visible. The person who is a custodian seems to have a more positive identity than a janitor. A sanitary engineer carries an aura of importance not afforded a garbage collector. The titles, while not usually increasing paychecks commensurately, appear to increase the sense of personal worth and self-esteem. Isn't it sad that we engage in face-saving word games or euphemisms, instead of acknowledging the importance of all work?

No matter how demeaning the task, no matter how deep the sense of alienation, we must work. We consider ourselves fortunate if we have jobs that give us a personal sense of satisfaction as well as a means of financial support. Freud said that the basic requirements of man are to love and to work. Modern men and women seem to find great difficulty in doing either, to any great degree of satisfaction or fulfillment. They have lost the joy of earning a self!

Technological advancements in recent years have given rise to new problems related to work. One of these is the problem of alienation. In the early years of our history, when our country was being settled, people worked and were identified by a particular product. The blacksmith had tangible evidence of his labor and often owned his own shop. The seamstress produced a garment that she had constructed from start to finish. The farmer grew food primarily for his family and sold extra produce to townspeople. Our ancestors saw the need for their products and derived a sense of satisfaction from the completion of the tasks involved. The product itself was important and gave the worker a real sense of identity and self-worth.

Today, most people have no finished product to look upon with satisfaction. Many workers on an assembly line rarely experience completing a product from start to finish. Some office workers' individual contributions are often lost in the shuffle of paperwork. Too many civil servants learn to serve the system rather than service their clients' needs. And, many teachers must teach to the test rather than developing the minds of their students. So the paycheck becomes the prime motivating factor for working.

Yet, most of us yearn for meaning in our work beyond a paycheck. We want to feel as if we are contributing to something, that the fruits of our labor have some meaning for humankind. We want to make our mark and have it recognized. The steel worker in Terkel's *Working* says, "Sometimes out of pure meanness, when I make something, I put a little dent in it. I like to do something to make it really unique. Hit it with a hammer."

How sad that the steelworker cannot channel his energy in a more positive direction. How sad that the uniqueness of his product should be a dent. Suppose that some way could be found for him to contribute more creatively to his work? He would then feel a sense of pride and fulfillment through the efforts of his labor.

The Terkel book abounds with the dimly concealed discontent many of us feel for our jobs, illustrates the extent of our frustrations, and the depth of our feelings of alienation:

> The blue collar blues are more bitterly sung than the white collar moans. 'I'm a machine' says the spot welder. 'I'm caged' says the bank teller and echoes the hotel clerk. 'I'm a mule' says the steelworker.' 'A monkey can do what I do' says the receptionist. 'I'm an object' says the fashion model. Blue collar and white call upon the identical phrase 'I'm a robot'
> (p. xxxvii).

A friend of mine told me the story of his mother who had worked on an assembly line in Detroit for much of her life. The job was hard physical labor; she sewed rugs for cars, and her hand became misshapen from pulling the heavy material through the sewing machine. She hated the job but loved working at the plant. She enjoyed being part of the group and loved the opportunity for social interaction. My friend is convinced that his mother had a deep sense of personal worth which was directly attributable to the feeling of having belonged in the work group. In a sense, that group had many of the elements of a deeply caring community.

The story illustrates the human need for respect, which is often gratified or frustrated through work. My friend's mother's need for respect and belonging was satisfied by her work group of peers. The spot welder in *Working*, however, feels frustration rather than gratification with his job:

> You really begin to wonder. What price do they put on me? Look at the price they put on the machine. If that machine breaks down, there is somebody out there to fix it right away. If I break down, I'm just pushed over to the other side until another man takes my place. The only thing they have on their minds is to keep that line running (p. 160).

The work environment itself seems to affect one's identity and sense of esteem. A supportive environment satisfies our need for respect from others. When others respect us, we seem better able to respect ourselves, although this is not always so. Two different questions are posed in the linking of respect and self-respect. One is, "How do I think and feel about myself?" and the other is, "How do others think and feel about me?" It is possible for persons to have a high opinion of their own worth and to believe that others think highly of them also, when, in fact, they do not. Those whose esteem is not reality-based don't even know they don't know: they listen to their own self-serving inner voices; they see what they want to see and hear what they want to hear. Such persons do not have positive self-esteem; otherwise, they would be willing to listen and to hear what their co-workers think and feel and not to be so fearful of others' possible criticism.

Respect from peers on the job is an important component of the working world. Many individuals experience difficulty in keeping a job simply because they cannot or will not conform to the expectations of their peers. The worker in a factory, for example, must learn a certain work pace. He cannot be an unproductive worker that his co-workers must do some of his job; nor can he be a "rate-buster." He must learn how to navigate the culture in which he works.

I once worked in a factory that manufactured spark plugs. Work began at 7 a.m. and ended at 3 p.m. I noticed, however, that a small group of women finished work every day at about 2 p.m. They would then sit outside the door, fanning themselves, gossiping, and passing away the time. "Why are they so privileged?" I inquired of the woman who worked next to me. She explained that they had agreed upon a certain quota of work to produce each day. When they had made "x" number of spark plugs, they quit working. They had carefully calculated the number that would cover the amount of piecework required plus the precise number of spark plugs to give them an extra bonus. "But if they work the extra hour, they can make even more plugs and even more money," said I in my naiveté. "Sure," my fellow worker told me. "But if you keep making more and more plugs every day, they'll come to expect you to produce more. The basic rate required will increase and the bonus will decrease. So they stop when they reach the agreed upon number."

How I envied those women who sat outside and got the cool breeze on a hot summer's day! Try as I might, I was never able to reach their quota. I learned from that factory experience that there is no upward mobility for expert workers on the assembly line; therefore, the experienced workers devised a system that worked for the financial good of all and preserved their perks: sociability.

In many working environments, the peer group is similar to a family setting. People care about one another, assist each other in times of trouble. It's as if the quality of the relationship makes up for the sense of alienation, which often seems present in the actual work. Creative processes, which might once have been expended upon the product, are extended to the maintenance of social relationships. In such settings, there is a spirit of camaraderie that makes the work bearable. When this attitude prevails, there seems to be a sense of belonging that is deeply satisfying to those in the group. The sense of well-being is translated into more pride in a job well done.

Many persons, however, do not perceive their jobs as a source of pride or as fulfilling but as extremely boring and restricting. They don't find much personal satisfaction in their work. The working day seems endless. Nor do they feel respected for the job completed. Some engage in mindless behavior to relieve the monotony. In the spark plug factory, boredom was relieved by the appearance of Leon, a man who collected scraps of unused clay. He would arrive pushing a huge cart on wheels, and he always had a joke or a bit of gossip to be passed on from another department. Leon was a bright spot in the day for all of us. Boredom seems increasingly to be a symptom of human work, regardless of the kind of job one holds, unless people are able to exercise some freedom on the job.

To a larger extent than we realize, we are the architects of our own work experience. What can we do to make our work more interesting and satisfying? I'm thinking of a toll gate attendant at Exit 16W on the New Jersey Turnpike. He gave a piece of candy to those who stop at his booth along with a receipt or change. I found myself changing lanes, if I could, when I saw that he was on duty. The piece of candy makes me feel special; somehow it becomes a lucky omen for the day. I have heard others, who have experienced this phenomenon, express similar feelings. That toll gate attendant has found a way, apparently, to relieve the monotony of his job and to bring himself into relationship with others.

Franklin Watkins, mail carrier, says about his job:

You make the job pleasant or you don't...It depends on your personality. You talk to people, you don't see them for a few days, you ask about them. The old people, they get a letter from their children and you see the expression on their faces. That makes you feel you accomplished something. that makes you content. Mr. Watkins said he was concerned about errors, as are most of the postal employees who have been with the service some time...working for supervisors who appear 'hell bent for production' he does not know where it will all lead...The only thing I'm sure about,' the postman said, 'is me' (Jaynes, 1978:35).

Mr. Watkins has found a way to make his job meaningful. He feels that he is doing something useful and productive. He chooses not to be bored with his job. He chooses to do his job well. Mr. Watkins probably knows now the results of "supervisors who appear 'hell bent for production' [and] where it will all lead" due to the national publicity about our postal system. Postal employees across the country have expressed their dissatisfaction with their jobs by killing their supervisors and co-workers.

There are many people who view their work as a way to avoid boredom. A job fills a day with things to do. They don't have to make many choices. They are told what to do each day; the job is a place to go. Such people are often restless on vacations or on weekends and can't wait to get back on the job. Forced retirement is a serious problem for these individuals. They don't know how to play or how to seek out other interests in life. Often they experience a terrible sense of guilt when not working; they feel worthless. The period of adjustment to retirement is difficult for them. They seem unable to permit themselves to enjoy life in the absence of work. We read in the obituary columns of the deaths of the recently retired. It's as if they wither away in the absence of what they perceive as productivity.

Workaholic is a word that has entered our modern vocabulary. The workaholic frequently uses his job as an excuse to avoid problems in his life. The individual who has an unhappy home life spends long hours on the job in order to escape personal problems. The person who is afraid to play uses work to avoid vacations; he says he doesn't have time to relax and enjoy himself. The aspiring writer complains of voluminous paper work that distracts him from writing. Work for these individuals becomes a shield to be used against life and living.

Many persons apparently work for the sheer joy of creating something. They find that their jobs fulfill their human need for activity and stimulation. They seem to have learned how to integrate work as just one part of their lives. I think of an eighty-year-old friend who retired from teaching when he was in his late fifties. He began to compose and arrange music shortly after his retirement. His work found an eagerly receptive market, and soon he had no financial problems. My friend enjoys his composing and continues to work every day of his life. His work does not possess him; he is in control of it. He stops to watch the birds, to go shopping, and to visit with friends who stop by.

He is an active letter writer, corresponding with old friends and family members who live in various parts of the country. His letters are thoughtful, witty, and carry a message of caring. My friend is a learned man who recently embarked upon rereading the classics, which he had enjoyed as a young man. He also avidly reads the newly published books that strike his fancy. He lives a rich, full life.

Of course, the facts that my friend is self-employed and is an artist make his situation a little different. However, he has accepted responsibility for doing something that is meaningful to him. Often we put work outside that arena for which we accept responsibility, believing that work is what we do for the boss or the corporation, not something we do for ourselves. Impoverishing ourselves with that attitude brings about lowered self-esteem. As we fail to exercise our autonomy, we become increasingly unaware of the degree to which it even exists. To some extent, life satisfaction is different from just working on a specific task or a job. In fact, job satisfaction is related to life satisfaction.

To improve the quality of working and, thus, the quality of our lives, perhaps we should ask ourselves some questions, "What can I do to make my labors more satisfying?" "What is it that I value about working?" "What do I look forward to doing on the weekend or upon retirement?" "Can I do some of it now?" "What does this job do for me?" "How do I feel at work?" "What contributes to my feeling of being up or down?" "What kinds of things can I do about it?" "How does my self-esteem rise or fall as I'm working?" "How can I intervene in that?"

If it is indeed the lot of humankind to live by the sweat of the brow, perhaps we need to find our own ways to enrich the quality of life lived while working and by learning to actually esteem ourselves more highly. Our problem seems to be less one of freeing ourselves from the need to work and more one of transforming the experience of work. Instead of looking forward to retirement or celebrating "Thank God, it's Friday!" perhaps we can learn in small and effective daily ways to celebrate this day, at work as well as at play.

CHAPTER VII

GETTING BACK TO BASICS

"GETTING BACK TO BASICS" is the cry bombarding us from the educational community today. Getting back to basics usually means more of the 3R's: more structure, more formality, and more "making them learn" and "passing the tests." The proponents of getting back to basics sometimes seem oblivious to the fact that nothing is more fundamental, beyond food, shelter, and clothing, than the basic human needs for love, respect, belonging, and relating. Paramount is the need to develop whole healthy human beings. We tend to trust that this will happen automatically, that perhaps the psychological aspect of human development has no place in the school curriculum. Yet, how we learn makes all the difference in using productively what we learn.

In the process of living and learning, we form self-esteem and a sense of self. Most learning is indirect; yet, all learning has lifelong effects. Children are naturally curious, astute observers, and eager learners. My grandson Adam was four when he was on Captiva Island, Florida, with us. While listening to a group of adults identifying the names of birds, one said, "That's an egret!" Adam interrupted him with, "It's an ibis." Asked how he knew that, he replied, "Because my grandfather told me so." He was right.

Children need to be affirmed for something they do well or know, but they have to know inside themselves that they know and that they did something well. They know when they are being praised for "nothing." Children learn all the time and from every aspect of their lives, including Little League, church, and extracurricular activities, not just in a formal school setting. My grandson Allen's participation in church activities has led to his becoming the youngest deacon. He is proud of his achievement, which is now a source of his self-esteem and sense of responsibility. An important learning for him is the fact that he earned his title; it was not given to him. Many of us were fortunate in having had good experiences in school systems, which fostered a positive sense of psychological well-being. Others of us, however, carry deep emotional scars as a result of our educational process.

A study of college graduates illustrates the need for becoming more focused upon developing psychologically healthy human beings. That research was based on 68 Haverford men who were studied since their freshman year in the early 1960s. The findings seem to indicate that the highest achievers turn out, ten or fifteen years later, to be less competent and less mature than students who didn't achieve as well academically.

Douglas A. Heath, Professor of Psychology at Haverford College, cautions that these findings are not conclusive. There is, however, considerable evidence to suggest that so-called "non-academic" factors such as moral values, character development, and interpersonal skills may be more important to a graduate's growth and success as an adult than the intellectual accomplishments most colleges emphasize.

The research indicates that men with higher verbal aptitude, in comparison with their classmates, had an inaccurate understanding of themselves, tended to be more self-centered, and had "tense and distant" relationships at work. They believed the people to whom they were closest did not understand them well. As adults, the men with higher verbal aptitude had not learned the empathic skills necessary for understanding and relating to others.

The men who best met their college department's expectations of intellectual growth had, as adults, less stable identities, were less well integrated and autonomous, had less mature relationships with their colleagues, and had less intimate relations with their wives. In fact, increasing quantitative aptitude was directly related to increasing interpersonal immaturity. Men who had received honors in college, compared with those who had not, seemed quite removed psychologically from the practical and realistic problems of the day. Twelve years after graduation the honor students were more abstract, more depressed, and less aggressive than others in the sample (Jacobsen, 1977).

That study suggests that highly educated, academically successful college graduates do not become competent and well-integrated adults on the basis of their academic skills alone. As much attention needs to be paid to developing the moral and social aspects of their character as to the development of their intellect. "Society will increasingly demand adaptive skills such as a capacity for self-education and close interpersonal relationships," says Professor Heath. "Colleges should avoid over-valuing academic preparation at the expense of psychological development...should not go off on a narrow, career educational vocationalism or they will undercut the potential for helping their students become more mature and therefore more adaptable people later on" (Jacobsen, 1977).

The implications of this study are clear for every level of education, not just for college students. Suppose we paid serious attention to the emotional development of children when they first attended school? Might it not be possible for us to educate human beings who esteem themselves more highly, who are able to cope with the stresses of life, who are happy and productive?

We know a great deal about how to create learning environments which foster maximum academic learning and which experiences nurture healthy psychological development. It is possible to learn academic skills as one also learns to become an independent, self-directed, and interpersonally mature human being.

In our interaction with the important people in our lives, such as teachers who respect and esteem us as is, we develop feelings of worthiness and esteem. An accepting, nurturing, challenging environment enables the developing self to thrive and grow joyously, reaching out for all of life. In a rigid, closed, punishing environment the self becomes impoverished and stifled. Often the result of an impoverished self is negative self-esteem, a numbness and fear of living. This defeated self makes do with what comes its way, is fearful of taking risks, and is less able to live happily and productively. The quality of the relationship between teacher and student is one of the most important elements in a nurturing learning environment. The relationship can facilitate learning, and help the student perceive self as a worthwhile human being, or the relationship can be debilitating, making the student view self as a failure.

These negative feelings are the result of small, daily incidents that erode the self-respect of a child. I visited a school where a small boy sat slumped behind a desk, turning pages of a workbook in a disheartened way. Since it was after school, it was obvious that the boy was serving some kind of detention. I stopped to chat with him. As we talked, a teacher passed by and looked into the room. "*Who* are you talking to?" she asked. "Oh, B. J.!" as she answered her own question. "Look at him! He's the only kid in school who would be dumb enough to wear a flannel shirt when it's 88 degrees outside." She walked on, oblivious to the results of her remarks. Burt's eyes dulled, and he slumped more deeply into his chair.

I didn't know what crime B. J. had committed in order to receive detention, but I saw a crime committed by the teacher's thoughtless remarks and the results. The child felt the venomous sting; tears filled his eyes. Referring to his shirt, "It's a birthday present," he said to me in a small voice. How can one desensitize the effect of such a toxin? "It's a beautiful color," I said and smiled. My stomach churned at the insensitivity of the teacher. The child was helpless and had no direct way to respond. He sat, internalizing the hurt.

The tragedy lies in the fact that the teacher was unaware of the effect of her behavior. In shaming and humiliating the child, she had failed to recognize him as a person. It was an impersonal and unfeeling expression of the teacher's lack of sensitivity and awareness. Not only teachers, but all adults, especially parents, other authority figures, and peers, are guilty of what Alice Miller calls "soul murder" when they shame, humiliate, and abuse other human beings, especially young children.

This incident illustrates the lack of a nurturing environment. What happens to the child if he experiences this negative kind of treatment day after day? He can become alienated, insensitive even to himself. School becomes a burden; study is a chore. There is no excitement or joy in learning. He may become bored. When a student is bored, he engages in schoolwork half-heartedly, if at all. He is threatened and cajoled into performance. He is stimulated, prodded. He is rewarded and punished. Sometimes the child strikes back by becoming hostile and aggressive. More often, he becomes passive, lethargic, and disinterested. He is fighting to save the integrity of the self, but the struggle is viewed by others as a defiance of authority. He is labeled as uncooperative, a troublemaker, dumb, or stupid.

In a nurturing relationship, the teacher respects a child, accepts him as unique and worthwhile. When a child is respected, he is shown that he is deeply cared for, that his individuality is respected, that his total being is accepted without reservation or qualification. The task of finding a way to communicate our respecting and caring to children is a difficult one. Yet, there are many teachers who respond warmly, tenderly, and humanely to all.

Good teachers seem to know how to encourage children to recognize, express, and experience their own uniqueness. They create interesting environments with variety and diversity to provide stimulation and challenge. They issue invitations to children to be themselves. Children who are free to be themselves seldom violate the trust placed in them. My student and friend, Clare, was such a teacher. Her third grade classroom was exciting, vital, and always filled with projects the students had made. The children were proud to show visitors the quality of their work. I could feel the excitement and the love of learning present in her classroom. When I analyzed what was different about Clare's classroom, I realized that she always drew upon the best in each student. Praise was given when deserved; mistakes were acknowledged as the basis for further learning. No child was ever demeaned. All problems were openly shared and discussed as solutions were sought by students and teacher together. I've encountered many of Clare's students who are now adults; they remember her with love and affection. Many say her class was a turning point in their lives.

As Clare demonstrated, one of the ways we can help children to experience their uniqueness is to really listen to them and to respond in a way that shows we hear what they are saying. It is difficult to respond with deep empathy at a moment's notice. But we can open up the lines of communication. We can let students know that we care and that we really do want to hear what they have to say to us.

I have observed, over the years, a unique tool which I have taught teachers to use as a method of communication: journal writing. "These sixth graders are so shy," one teacher said to me. She related that many of them had deep personal problems that they couldn't talk about in class. So, she asked if they'd like to keep journals and share their writings with her. At first, only a few journals appeared on her desk. As she read them and wrote little responses, more and more of the children became involved in the process. They began to say things to each other in writing that they were unable to say in the larger impersonal setting. By the end of the year, every child was keeping a journal. She considers journaling to be the most effective teaching she's ever done. She had learned to listen to students. As I visited schools, I became aware that many of my students who were teachers were using the journaling technique at all grade levels. There seemed to be a quality of caring in the classes that used journals. The educational setting appeared to be more personal, and students were more involved with their own learning.

My case study of Jane is recorded and discussed in Daniel Prescott's book, *The Child in The Educative Process* (1957); he learned of my work from Julie Gordon under whom I studied journaling at the New Jersey State Department of Education and had practiced it with public school children. With a grant from W. T. Grant, Julie was able to provide me with a two-year fellowship to complete my doctorate (1968) in the Child Study Institute, founded by Dr. Prescott, at the University of Maryland.

What is it about the journaling process that seems to be so effective? What is the magic in journaling? Journaling became the core of my doctoral dissertation.

I had long been interested in the work of the psychologist Sidney Jourard. He believes that being one's real self is most essential to the development of a healthy personality. In our society, we are punished not only for the things we actually do, but also for what we think, feel, or want. We learn to hide our feelings in order to present the concept we want others to have of us. As a result, we often experience alienation from ourselves. A way to get in touch with the inner self, Jourard wrote (1964), was to disclose oneself fully to another human being. This meant telling our innermost thoughts, our deepest secrets, our doubts and despairs, as well as our joys. In the process of revealing our true self, we come to understand, value, and accept who and what we are. When we love and respect ourselves, the stage is set for becoming a fully developed, healthy human being.

This process seemed to be what was happening in the journal classes. Kids were revealing themselves; they actually were engaged in what Jourard calls self-disclosure. I decided to explore this idea to discover if self-esteem could be elevated through the use of journals in my work with children and teachers throughout the State of New Jersey.

I worked with sixth grade students for my doctoral studies and discovered that they were able to surface their concerns and problems as they wrote in their journals. In the process they began to hear themselves; they seemed to get in touch with who and what they were. The process was a healing one for many of them. One student reported, "You can tell the journal everything, and it listens to you. It never repeats what you say, and it never talks back. Most people never listen to you. The journal helps get the steam out of your system."

There appeared to be value in thinking about a situation, writing it down, rereading it. Some of the children said they could laugh about a problem when they reread their entries several days later. What had seemed so earth-shaking at the moment became silly in retrospect. "How could I get upset over something so silly?" asked one girl. She had described an argument she had had with her mother about what she should wear to school.

Most of the children's journal entries were written very simply, but the ideas and insights developed were profound. Some examples:

Today I am looking very pretty, and the children tell me so. I have a sister, and she is always in trouble. I feel sorry for her. I have two nieces, and they are my sister's children. When she leaves them with my mother, my mother has eleven children and five grandchildren, and my mother has trouble, boy!

Today I walked into class and "S" started laughing at my shoes for no reason. How can I tell the teacher without "S" finding out I told her? I wore different shoes because my mother wanted to wear mine (we wear the same size). I can't think of nothing else.

For dinner we had hamburgers. My mother died, and so it's really hard on my father and so he always picks on me.

I want to tell you that I am very pleased to write. This way I can express my feelings, and I am helping you in your work, which pleases me also. Have a good day! Please give me some advice about boys in your free time.

I'm kind of worried about conference time because I talk a little extra in class.

This boy wants to fight me, and I don't want to fight so I run. And he can not run so good.

My mother made me wear these ugly socks, and they are tan and I have on white and red. I am mad; don't bother me today.

Yesterday Miss J wouldn't let me get my gym suit, and I got a red mark in gym. She really made me mad, and I felt like calling her a bad name. But I forgot that she was a teacher and I was a child and I could've got kicked out of school, but by the end of the day we made up.

Those are just a few of the entries made by the children. Their journals revealed many of the concerns we all have in common. They spoke of loneliness, guilt, anxiety, and anger and about fears of rejection, failure, and dying. The surfacing of their fears and concerns appeared to have a cathartic effect upon these children. Moreover, through the process of keeping a journal, they came to value and respect themselves in new and different ways. They felt less alone, and they got in touch with their own uniqueness.

The nurturing quality of a good teacher is much the same as the nurturing quality of a good parent. When children go to school, each comes into contact with a large number of new individuals. Their world is expanded, and they have to learn to "make it" on their own. This experience can be a very happy and fulfilling one for the child or it can be devastating. It depends very much upon the various teachers that the child encounters along the way. Doesn't it seem strange that we prize the academic achievements of teachers so highly and yet seem to pay little attention to their interpersonal skills? Teachers must take exams that give an indication of intellectual achievement and reveal whether they've mastered a body of academic knowledge. We don't seem to be particularly interested in the ways they interact with others. It is only when the behavior is deviant in the extreme that we become alarmed.

In a nearby community, there had been a woman who taught seventh and eighth grade children for many years. At that age, children are already aware of each other and make overtures to one another. This teacher became very upset by any evidence of boy-girl relationships. On class trips, she would not permit the boys and girls to sit together. They could not walk down a hall together, and she was at the evening dances to see that they danced at arm's length. Her students tell story after story about how negatively this teacher had made them feel. The young girl who held a boy's hand as they left a ball game was lectured severely the next day: "If you keep on with this behavior you'll grow up to be a prostitute," said the teacher. The girl was devastated, felt demeaned, thought something was wrong with her. She was afraid to tell her parents, believing that they too would fault her behavior. After a few years the children learned how to cope with that teacher, Mrs. "X"; she became a legend, and they warned each other about her idiosyncrasies. They finally figured out that there was something wrong with her, not with them.

In the meantime, Mrs. "X" had emotionally scarred a large number of children. They had been made to believe that physical expressions of caring were dirty and disgusting. Fortunately, most teachers are not like Mrs. "X." They care about their students, worry about them, and do the best job that they can. Sometimes when I work with students, who are studying to become teachers, I ask them to write about the teachers who made the most impact upon their lives.

The message is almost always the same. They remember the teachers who had a positive effect and also the ones who affected them negatively. The ones they remember positively affirmed them as human beings. Over and over they say, "Mrs. 'A' really liked me. I got interested in learning in her class," or "Mrs. 'B' gave me a glimpse of what I could be. I never knew there were so many options," or "Mrs. 'C' helped me to feel successful. I never felt inferior in her class."

The good teachers remembered were the ones who seemed to know how to alternate play and work, study and games. They seemed to know how to encourage special talents, to recognize when teachers' made special efforts to help them. Nurturing relationships in the learning environment produces a sense of warmth, respect, and acceptance. The student is then able to acquire the joy of working and of learning to do something well.

At no time are children more ready to learn than when they first come to school. They are eager to make things; they want to share in constructing and planning. They attach themselves to the teacher and to the parents of other children. They watch and imitate policemen, actresses, carpenters, media characters, and athletes. They play actively and strenuously. Good teachers harness that energy and put it to productive use, leading the child to discover and learn, to experience success. Good teachers help students gain a sense of well-being, a joy in being real. When teachers respect and esteem children, they create an environment to facilitate growth for students to become psychologically healthy, which is necessary for intellectual learning.

Isn't it difficult for a teacher to esteem and value each child? After all, classrooms are large, and there are often twenty-five or more students with whom the teacher interacts. Yes, of course, it is difficult. But I have observed that it is more difficult to run authoritarian classrooms where teachers are the disciplinarians, meting out punishment, lecturing, deciding who talks and who doesn't, and assigning grades for academic and behavioral skills. In authoritarian classrooms, the teachers shoulder the burden of responsibility; they become responsible for students' learning, for their behavior. It usually becomes a contest to see who will win and who will lose. By sheer force and threat, teachers can make students do homework, take exams, control them through report cards and grades. An authoritarian style is very draining and debilitating for both teachers and students.

When teachers permit students to enter into the planning for learning and into the management of the classroom, the students begin to feel a stake in their own learning. When responsibility is shared, the need for disciplining and punishing is diminished. Students are then too busy doing exciting things to consciously misbehave. Students are also more likely to become future contributors to decision-making processes when they are encouraged to engage in them in school.

Creating an exciting learning environment does take a lot of work. However, students learn to share in that preparation. They assist the teacher in bringing to class all kinds of books and materials for experiments once they become interested. They begin to say what excites them. And, they work harder than the teacher would have required.

Just as infants must learn to walk, to feed themselves, so must children learn the academic skills needed for them to become functional in our society. They need to learn how to read, how to write, how to compute, and how to relate. A master teacher assists learners to do it for themselves, helps them to learn how to feed themselves intellectually. Learning is achieved in a supportive atmosphere when students are encouraged to experiment, to risk, to be kind to one another. When they are praised for positive achievements, learners feel affirmed, value themselves, and trust that they can do it again.

Students who are spoon-fed learn to wait for that feeding, to become dependent upon the person doing the feeding. When teachers assign pages and chapters and homework sheets, they seem to be trying to "spoon" in knowledge quickly and efficiently. Learners soon learn to obediently open their mouths and to take in large chunks of facts, but they don't digest it very well because the required digestive enzymes may be missing. Just as human stomachs accept and process or reject and eliminate food, so does the human mind. It all depends upon the inner environment's content and readiness.

A great teacher knows how to make maximum use of teachable moments. Between the ages of six and eleven, for example, children are more ready to learn than they ever have been in their lives. They want to know how things are made and how they work. Alert teachers have materials available in the classroom. Erector sets make wonderful bridges and skyscrapers. Scraps of material, scissors, needle and thread, and dolls to dress are available for the aspiring designers. Batteries, wires, and bells encourage electrical experiments. Vases and bowls may be made while playing with clay. Scissors and scraps of paper or greeting card cutouts invite the artistic spirits to make collages. Boxes of old finery suggest "dress-up" and creative play. Giving a wide variety of available choices works naturally with the energy surging within children. Developing muscles are strengthened and fine talents are encouraged during the manipulation of scissors, pencils, and crayons. Rocks and seashells as well as books on these subjects invite students to identify and classify. The learning is organic; yet the environment has been carefully structured by the teacher. Children begin to add interesting things collected on family trips or found in the home. When learners ask questions and teachers consider questions important to the learning process, students are affirmed. If they are told that their questions are stupid, that they already know the answer, or that they wouldn't have any questions if they had really listened or had studied, they soon stop questioning. When learners are praised for their efforts, they feel good about themselves and eagerly go on to the next adventure in learning. But if they are told that they are making a mess or that they are clumsy or stupid, many shut down; some actually do become clumsy and stupid, obeying the self-fulfilling prophecy.

Adolescence is a disturbing period for most youngsters. Their bodies are changing rapidly. They become awkward, unaccustomed to the feet and arms which suddenly seem too large and unfamiliar. They are often shy, feel agonizingly different, and each blemish on the face seems like a spotlight. Adolescents seem particularly vulnerable and require teachers who are patient and understanding of the fact that a thirteen-year-old can behave like an adult one day and like a five-year-old the next.

Great teachers make it permissible for them to slip back into childish behavior and don't overly punish or criticize them. Since an important need for the adolescent is the identification of heroes, good teachers fill their classrooms with biographies and films about all kinds of famous people: sports stars, artists, musicians, statesmen, scholars, inventors, and humanitarians. Adolescents are idealistic, seeking to form their own philosophy of life and so they are assisted by the alert teacher in exploring many different ways of living. These youngsters often become interested in causes, and so the teachable moment is capitalized upon by teachers who want to make learning meaningful for their students. However, there is a downside to adolescence.

"Mean girls" is not a new phenomenon in our society, but girls' inhumanity to girls is now being studied and given public attention. In an article by Margaret Talbot in *The New York Times Magazine* (February 24, 2002), she reported on cruelty among girls. A Finnish professor interviewed eleven and twelve-year-old girls and found they are just as aggressive as young boys. While the girls did not engage in physical fights, their superior social intelligence enabled them to wage complicated battles with other girls aimed at damaging relationships or reputations. They left nasty messages or spread scurrilous rumors via e-mail or made friends with one girl to revenge another, gossiped about a girl just loud enough to be overheard. All such slurs are intended to create "in" girls and "out" girls where the "in" girls feel powerful at others' expense. Psychologists are now calling such behavior "relational aggression," which has become a nationwide problem, particularly among fifth and sixth graders.

Both my granddaughters, Chelsea and Alice, have suffered from other girls' cruelty. Their self-esteem is secure enough so they discuss their relational problems with their parents and with me. They now realize that girls' mean behavior has nothing to do with themselves but has everything to do with mean girls' lack of respect and esteem for themselves and for others.

After parents and peers, few adults have as much influence upon the young as do the teachers in their lives. Great teachers esteem learners and require students to esteem each other; they nurture and affirm all as worthy human beings while assisting them in the learning process; they support their efforts, but do not do the work for them. The great teacher creates a stimulating learning environment full of wonder and questions, which leads to curious students. There is a sensitivity and awareness in such teachers, which enable them to engage students in meaningful activity; often, they recognize precisely the options needed to be explored at particular moments.

The accomplished pianist performs his art with relative ease; the great basketball player seems to just reach up and drop the ball into the basket. As we watch, it seems so easy and effortless. That's the way it is when a person performs well. This is particularly true in the teaching profession. The great teachers make room for students to feel responsible for their own learning; they don't claim ownership of their students' achievements. Their satisfaction comes from seeing students become self-directed, self-motivated, and knowledgeable but psychologically healthy human beings.

Great teachers help their students deal with the confusing, the difficult, and the unexpected. They have learned to see with their hearts, to listen with their inner ear, as well as with their intellect. They know that students aren't sponges who passively soak up understanding. Understanding is developed through the facts of day-to-day living. While exploring these facts, testing them, talking about them, and discovering what needs to be discovered, students grow in understanding. In addition, all teachers must learn to nurture self-esteem along with teaching academic skills. "We see, then, that what students need from teachers, if they are to grow in self-esteem is respect, benevolence, positive motivation, and education in essential knowledge and vital skills" (Branden, 1994, p. 221). Of course, teachers have to have their own positive self-esteem in order to create an environment for their students to flourish.

Learning is often the result of hard work; it entails a certain amount of risking, groping, and griping. Mistakes are made, dead-ends and detours occur. The sensitive, intuitive teachers take all this "stuff" and somehow weave it into a fabric of understanding, helping students to develop intellectually as well as guiding them in experiencing a feeling of success and self worth.

Educators are forever looking for panaceas "out there" to improve learning, but testing is the bottom-line. "Thorough and Efficient" was New Jersey's mandated system of education, but T&E turned out to be just another "trial and error" approach. To acquire basic skills in obtaining information, solving problems, thinking critically, and communicating effectively are the desired outcomes of the T&E educational goal. This is indeed a noble goal and would provide our children with a foundation for a lifetime of learning. No one can quarrel with this goal. It is what we wish for all of us: to be able to think critically, especially.

The danger is how this goal is to be achieved. When educational guidelines are vague and inconsistent, a "skills" approach that does not include content standards reduces the academic knowledge base for problem solving and thinking critically. Testing for knowledge is important, but we mustn't be carried away with teaching only what we can test. Learning how to learn is among the most essential learning for a lifetime. It must not be sacrificed for a test score. It is a truism that students also learn from what we do as well as what we say and how we say it.

The excellent teacher is a healthy human being, teaching by example through exhibiting maturity, tolerance, and enthusiasm and by having the ability to express and handle feelings appropriately. Teachers make visible to their students who they are so they teach what they are. Students learn through the actions, attitudes, and atmosphere in the schools. They learn to relate to a wide variety of people when they see older children, teachers, and principals relating well to each other. When the people around students are really feeling good about themselves, when they are alive and learning and growing along with their students, it becomes contagious. Students catch it and learn it too.

"Let's get back to basics," the critics cry. What could be more basic than helping human beings learn to prize themselves so they could lead growthful, productive, and satisfying lives.

CHAPTER VIII

AS YE SOW...

THE FRAIL ELDERLY COUPLE seated at the table next to mine had entered the restaurant hesitantly. They studied the menu for a long time and finally, after much deliberation, ordered carefully and haltingly, the special of the day — meat loaf for $3.95. Were they counting their pennies and savoring this occasional night out — maybe trying to make the ritual last? I smiled as I watched their pleasure, saw his hand gently cover hers.

The waitress came to serve them and the lady said, "Oh my!" as a huge platter of meat loaf was placed before her. Clearly overwhelmed by the size of the portion, she was able to eat a little of it. Returning to clear the table, the waitress noticed the half-consumed meal, laughed, and said in a loud voice, "You're a naughty girl. You didn't finish your dinner. Next time we will have to give you a kiddie plate."

The waitress seemed totally oblivious to the content of her remark, unaware that she was speaking to the diner as if she were a child. Did a shadow of pain pass over the elderly woman's face as she quietly replied, "You give large portions here." Or, was it my pain at the waitresses' thoughtless and rude remark? I became interested in the little tableau and watched the waitress as she moved from table to table. I heard her addressing both the elderly and the very young in exactly the same way, with a loud teasing voice, as if they were idiots and couldn't comprehend what she was saying. It seems a common occurrence in our society to treat both the very old and the very young as if they were deaf and dimwitted.

When I was hospitalized recently, the curtain was drawn about my roommate's bed. The nurses came and went, and I heard her addressed as "honey" and "dear." "Eat your breakfast like a good girl" and "Be a good dear and roll over" were the commands that floated over to me. How shocked I was to discover a woman in her eighties when the curtains were finally drawn back! I had assumed from the way she was being addressed that she was a child. How often we seem to equate old age with infantile behavior.

It is only in recent years that we have begun to seriously address the phenomenon of aging. This is probably due to the increasing number of elderly among us. At the time our constitution was written, life expectancy was in the 30s; a hundred years ago it was in the 40s. Today one can expect to reach age 75, and in the early 21st century, people over 65 will the in the majority, known as the graying of America. Many of us can reasonably expect to live to an older age.

What does it mean to be old? I have known people who seem to be old at thirty and young at seventy. Feeling old or projecting an image of being old seems to be symptomatic of withdrawal from life. When people say, "I feel a hundred years old today," they mean they're feeling depressed, tired, ill, or disturbed. An older person may say, "I feel young today," meaning, "I'm feeling cheerful, healthy, and full of well-being." Old has an unsavory connotation in our society. Young seems to automatically imply good and beautiful. We spend millions of dollars in the pursuit of perpetual youth — face lifts, cosmetics, hair coloring, and transplants. We seem to want to find the Fountain of Youth for our outward appearances. Often, though, we are forced to try to look younger even when we don't really wish to engage in this pursuit. The skills of a forty year old are often more marketable than those of a fifty year old, and so the fifty year old feels it is essential to look ten years younger in order to be employable.

A beautiful woman of fifty-five was interviewed on a TV show. She is a model but can't find much work because her hair is a lovely silver and there are wrinkles in the corners of her eyes. Our preoccupation with youth makes her a liability in the modeling marketplace. "We all grow old," she said, "but you wouldn't know it from looking at the magazines. They show only young faces. How can we expect our youth to look forward to aging when we act as if it were some terrible disease? Isn't it time we displayed a few models with aging faces? I feel vigorous, attractive, and full of life." I agree. Her face and figure have a stunning beauty and maturity reflecting an inner loveliness that only comes from a life well-lived, from learning who and what one is.

One of our great fears about growing old seems to be the fear that we will be rejected because of our non-youthful appearance. Is this because our society seems to value young looks above all else? When Ronald Reagan was campaigning for the presidency, we all knew that he was seventy years old. His medical records indicated that he was in excellent physical health. But it was the color of his hair that seemed to be of most interest to the media — never mind that he was a physically healthy specimen: Did he color his hair? Some reporters apparently became so obsessed with this notion that they confiscated his hair clippings to analyze and discover whether he did or didn't. What difference does it make? Did hair color help him to withstand the would-be assassin's bullet? Isn't mental alertness and physical fitness more important than hair color?

As I write this, I recall two separate encounters I had with people I had not seen in a long time. "When did you begin coloring your hair blonde?" asked an old schoolmate. When I said "Hello" to a woman who had been my supervisor in the elementary schools years and years ago, she didn't recognize me. "I haven't seen you since your hair turned gray," she said. I confess that I liked being called a blonde much better than I liked the reference to becoming gray. Yet, neither of these statements actually altered the color of my hair. It is what it is. However, blonde seemed to say young and gray screamed, *old*. How easily I fall into the trap of thinking old and young, despite all my striving to the contrary!

I am concerned about my appearance but became so accustomed to the hair color and skin tone of my youth that I didn't even notice when they changed — even though I look at myself in the mirror every day. I continue to see my familiar face and remain true to that reflected image. I faithfully wore the colors that suited me for so long and didn't even realize some were no longer attractive on me. I've learned that the colors which were once taboo for me now look great — so I'm wearing lots of purple, lavender, and turquoise. I would never have experimented with any of these colors if my daughters hadn't urged me to do so. I enjoy these little discoveries, these little changes; they seem more like me. I enjoy my daughters' participation in this process too. Not so long ago we shopped for clothes to get them ready for school. Now, they get me ready for school, often locating the best outfit for me to wear when teaching a seminar. I'm reminded once again of how the cycles of life come full circle. The energy I expended in helping them with their appearance is now being returned to me; now I am on center stage. I love it!

To the aging, the greatest compliment we seem able to give is, "You don't look your age," or "You're looking younger," instead of responding to their inner self. I suppose when people say, "You look ten years younger," they actually mean and are relating to the person's inner life. I think I look best when I'm excited by a relationship, by what's happening in the exchange between us. I know that I feel most alive when that's happening and the inner glow shines through. But when I feel rejected, not responded to or don't feel good about myself, the diminished me is apparent in my face. So age doesn't seem to be the critical factor in one's appearance; it's the quality of the inner life which becomes outwardly reflected.

It's this learning to pay attention to the inner self, to the inner life, that is so very important. If we can learn to do that effectively while young, aging then becomes a natural process.

How do we get in touch with that inner self? One way, I think, is through encountering our aloneness. Most of us are afraid of a universal aloneness, of being alone in a vast and unknown world as well as in our own unknown inner world. Then we cling to others — spouses, lovers, friends, or children. We feel abandoned when left alone by rejection, death, or separation, and we seek to avoid this terrible aloneness. We have learned to depend upon support from outside ourselves. As children, we looked to our parents, later to a lover, spouse, or job, and perhaps to our children to fill our felt emptiness and aloneness.

Being afraid of abandonment is a carryover from childhood. Young children have little source of support beyond parents. However, adults have many additional resources, if they would take advantage of them. The best support system for an adult is to learn to be one's own best friend; therefore, adults often really need time to be alone, to think, to contemplate, to filter the accumulated stuff of life.

I find self-renewal in periods of aloneness, but people often find it strange when they encounter me all by myself. Once I went to the Florida Keys. I wanted some time to work on my writing with no interruptions; I also wanted a pleasant environment. When I went to dinner that first evening, the hostess let me wait for a few minutes before she seated me. "Oh," she said, "I didn't realize that you were here all by your lonesome; I thought you were waiting for someone." I smiled and wanted to say, "I'm here alone, but I'm not lonesome." Of course, I didn't. As I looked around, I saw that I was the only person sitting alone in the dining room. The hostess became very solicitous of me and, throughout my stay, gave me the very best table where I could look out at the water. We became friends during that week because she'd stop to chat with me during the periods of slow activity. She found it difficult to deal with my aloneness; it was as if she were trying to shield me from it by somehow making us a pair.

Facing aloneness creates great anxiety for many of us. So we join groups, cling to our friends and families, do this and that, everything not to be alone. This is not to suggest that we do not need support groups or that group membership is not important. We are social beings and need contact with others. They need not be continually available, however. We need to get in touch with and cultivate periods of positive aloneness. Many people first encounter aloneness when the empty nest beckons, spouses die, or retirement occurs.

Perhaps we tend to equate being alone with not being loved. Is it that we're afraid that if we're seen alone people will view us as being undesirable, rejected, or unloved? Perhaps that is what we believe about ourselves. In our adolescent years, we suffer great anxiety about being a wallflower. Many of us can recall the awful fear of being chosen last for a team or of not being asked to dance. Could it be that part of the fear of being alone in old age is a re-enactment of those early wallflower feelings?

It seems that this developmental task of handling aloneness well becomes forcibly encountered in later life. Life is our teacher so, in our later years, we may have more wisdom, for we have more experiences and resources to draw upon. One of those resources is the ability to become more settled into ourselves and our spiritual core. I think we often find this center through growing more comfortable with our ultimate aloneness and by becoming more deeply in touch with our inner world.

For me, the most valuable device for getting in touch with my inner world has been through my journal. It's as if there is a pathway from my head and heart, leading to the empty journal pages. I pick up my pen and just let it all flow right onto the page. It really is that simple.

When I first began journal writing, the entries were stiff and little more than jottings of things done, places visited. As I kept it, learning to relax with pen in hand, my feelings and thoughts found their way onto the pages. As I reread my old journals, I am astonished to find much more rich imagery. I can hardly believe I wrote those entries. I become aware that my life was not dull and lackluster, that in every day occurrences, such as trips to the supermarket, I often saw and mentally recorded poignant vignettes of life. As I drove to classes, I often wrote mental letters or had mental dialogues with friends or even "told somebody off." There was much satisfaction in "sounding off" to myself. When I learned to record all this information, I began to learn to work productively with the material of my life.

In our culture, we seem to perceive the outer world as reality and our inner world of feelings, ideas, and fantasies as nonreality. Sometimes we label people crazy, if they do not share our notion of reality. In Eastern philosophies, there is a greater emphasis upon inner feelings and the inner life than in our Western society. I'm suggesting that our inner worlds are very real; they contain rich material from which we need to draw.

Often, though, we're afraid to reveal our anxieties, our angry, negative feelings, and our vulnerabilities. So, we hold them inside, sometimes refusing to even discuss these feelings with ourselves. I find that if I'm aware of my feelings, if I can say to myself honestly how I'm feeling, that my anxieties, doubts, and pain just disappear by themselves most of the time. Part of the aging process for me has been learning to confront these feelings. When I was younger, I carried grievances for years; now I don't harbor ill feelings. Rather than focusing upon what the outside world is doing to me, I'm more able to experience what's happening in my inner world and what I'm doing to me or making happen to me. Coming to terms with who I am, having a fuller sense of myself, being less at risk, finding more peace and serenity, looking more deeply within — this is what aging means to me.

As I explored my inner world, I discovered that I need not always do everything for myself, that it is OK to receive help and even to ask for it. On my travels, I saw a bumper sticker quoting the Beatles: "I get by with a little help from my friends." In recent years, I've received a little help from loving friends and from my family. The wonderful thing has been my observation of their joy in being able to give something to me when I can receive their offerings in the spirit in which they're given. Giving is often a very loving gesture – I think I've known that for a long time. I'm learning that receiving can also be a loving act.

I think of a friend who for many years gave generously of her time and money. People who visited the city were hosted and entertained by her; she loved caring for them and sharing what she had. There came a time, though, when her income abruptly ceased and she was forced to live on a limited budget. People she'd entertained found her not accepting their invitations to dine out, etc. because as she said, "I can't pay my own way." She seemed to forget how she'd paid in the past. She had a tremendous fear of becoming dependent, of not being able to pay back. It was difficult for her to accept anything; she wanted to be independent.

I believe we tend to confuse the words independent and self-reliant. Independence seems to imply "I don't need you. I can take care of myself." Independence sometimes leads to isolation. Self-reliance, on the other hand, seems to suggest, "I can take care of myself, but I'd like to include you." When we're self-reliant, we make our own observations and judgments, but we may also consult and listen to others' opinions and accept others' gifts. We do need to see with our own eyes, to hear with our own ears, but we can also value the help and opinions of others. Ultimately, our decisions must be our own, but they are reached wisely when we consider and value the opinions of those who love us.

I have heard older persons say, "I don't want to become dependent on my children." What does this statement really mean? Sometimes it reflects a financial insecurity which is particularly acute in this post 9/11 period we're living through. Sometimes it is the fear of spending one's life alone in a nursing home, deserted and unloved. Sometimes, though, some parents resist giving up the role of parent; they fear having their adult children minister to them in a parental way. It's as if the set role of the parent is to give and for the children to receive.

The old film *East of Eden* portrays John Steinbeck's touching story about a young boy's love for his father and his continuous striving for his father's approval. The father seems not able to see or feel his son's love, let alone return it. Then the father, a vigorous man played by Raymond Massey, is struck down by a stroke and is confined to bed. The boy (James Dean) is frantic with his feelings of helplessness and the unaccepting, unreturned love of his father. The young girl who loves the boy, played by Julie Harris, makes an impassioned plea to the father, "Oh please," she says, "let your son care for you. Give him some sign that you love him; let him do something for you." The final scene shows the father making a supreme effort to talk. We see the son bending over his father; at last he turns and says to his girlfriend, with tears streaming down his face, "He says to get rid of that old battle-ax nurse. He wants me to take care of him!" And then he takes a chair and sits by the bed, as if he will never move from the spot.

I suppose it is in childhood that we begin to have such negative feelings about the word *dependent*. Being young and dependent, we learn to cope with our parents by being submissive and perhaps resentful or rebellious. We seem to need to do this to maintain some sense of our own identity and integrity. As we grow older and enter into intimate relationships, our old learned patterns surface which we used for coping with our parents. We may have felt angry, hurt, rejected, abandoned, etc. Usually the emotion we fear most is the very one we finally express in a relationship. Past unresolved problems emerge — jealousy, possessiveness, fear of rejection, lack of self-esteem.

Sooner or later, these unresolved carryovers become a paramount issue in the relationship. I wonder if it is possible that we are attracted to some people because, at an unconscious level, we sense the opportunity to work out those unresolved issues. If they can't be resolved, we seek a new relationship and begin the process all over again. Sometimes it takes several intimate relationships before we can work through a problem.

Studies show that having intimate relationships helps to keep us healthy. In our society, we have many competing notions about what constitutes intimacy. Intimacy, to me, suggests the ability for two people to share deeply with each other, to explore their vulnerabilities and weaknesses, to share their joys and sorrows, knowing that no matter what terrible or wonderful thing has happened, the other will understand and be present. Intimacy may or may not include a sexual relationship. Some of the most intimate relationships are those found in friendship between people who do not engage in sexual intercourse at all.

Yet, sexual intercourse is often an important aspect of an intimate relationship. Aging need not curtail this activity; if people choose to engage in physical love making, they are able to do so well into old age. The early studies by Masters and Johnson, for example, reveal that an interest in and a capacity for sex are present in those eighty and beyond. The principal change in sexuality is a slower response. It may take a man longer to achieve an erection, but it can be maintained longer. Older women, too, may take longer to achieve a level of excitement but continue to be multi-orgasmic until the day they die.

One of the persistent myths about aging, though, is the belief that sex is not for the elderly. Our society prolongs this myth with endless jokes about the loss of sexuality as one grows older. I think we have many hazy notions about what constitutes sexuality; we seem to believe that it is merely the ability to perform. We have come to equate manliness or womanliness with the number of orgasms one can achieve. There is more to expressing sexuality than having orgasms, pleasant as that is. Being sexual can be hugging, kissing, or touching another person. In fact, intercourse may be a way of avoiding intimacy. Sometimes it's easier to have intercourse than it is to be open and vulnerable to another human being. We have much to learn about the quiet gentle ways of love making related to sexuality which don't seem to put undue emphasis upon performance.

My eighty-five-year-old mother-in-law died. When we began the sad task of packing her clothes to give to the church, we found two very short, sheer, bright red nightgowns in the underwear drawer. I said the first thing that popped into my head, "I wonder where those came from!" My niece looked at me and said, "From her boyfriend, I hope." We both smiled and reminisced about that loving relationship which had lasted for several years, terminating when he died a year before she did. Somehow, we, my niece and I, felt a little closer for having found those red nightgowns. It made Gram feel more real, too.

Dealing with the death of Gram was a strange experience for me. I had answered the telephone at 5 a.m. to hear a trembling young voice asking whether this was the Castner residence. I said, "Yes," and she said, "This is Warren Hospital." Pause. I knew immediately and said, "I guess you have bad news." I was feeling sorry for the obviously young nurse for the difficulty she was having with passing on the news. "Yes," she said, "Mrs. Castner just expired." Expired! What an odd word. I guess she was afraid to say died.

We had never spoken of death, my mother-in-law and I. I don't know how she felt about dying. Some of her friends who came to call remarked how full of life she had been and how much she enjoyed doing things. "Georgie always knew what was going on and kept up with the fashions," said one friend. Gram and my daughter Lisa had flown to Florida for a two week vacation just two months before she died. She had taken her fishing pole and had a wonderful time.

During her last month, though, she began to fail dramatically, filling with fluid. The doctor said that her heart was two and one-half times its normal size. She stayed in her own home as long as she could and went to the hospital just four days before her death. They said she had died in her sleep. I don't think she feared dying because she so much enjoyed living. She had a full life, not a deferred one. That she had prepared for her death was evident in both large and small ways. Her burial wishes had been expressed and honored; her estate was in legal order. As we packed her belongings, we found names on the bottoms and backs of various art objects. She had selected a little token for each family member as a remembrance of her.

As we lived through those days of funeral preparations, I suddenly realized that my children were drawing closer to me. They were asking questions that made me aware that they were thinking of the future and of my death, of how I wanted things to be. Then it really hit me — I am now the eldest female member of our immediate family. Another milestone in my life!

I have experienced the death of my grandparents, parents, aunts, uncles, and both in-laws. The grief surrounding many of those deaths was deep and painful, but I don't actually know what it is to die. I have had changes in my life that I have resisted; some of them felt like a dying. I have experienced rejection, learned to let go of my children, but I lived through all those events and today feel very much alive and well-loved. I think we most fear death when we have not really lived, when we feel we've missed something so life is incomplete, when we have unresolved, negative relationships.

Carl Rogers wrote a paper on "Growing Old or Older and Growing" (1980). He discussed what it was like for him to be seventy-five years old. His section about productivity was most astounding to me. In his last decade, he had turned out four books, some forty shorter pieces, and several films. He wrote (Fall, 1980):

> But for me this has been a fascinating ten years — full of adventurous undertakings. I have been able to open myself to new ideas, new feelings, new experiences, new risks. Increasingly I discover that being alive involves taking a chance, acting on less than certainty, engaging with life. All of this brings changes, and for me the process of change is life. I realize that if I were stable and steady and static, I would be a living death. So I accept confusion and uncertainty and fear and emotional highs and lows because they are a price I willingly pay for a flowing, perplexing, exciting life...So I am being honest when I say this has been the most exciting decade of my life...As a boy, I was sickly and my parents have told me that it was predicted that I would die young. This prediction has been proven completely wrong in one sense, but has come profoundly true in another sense...I believe that I will die young!

The elixir of life is mental activity and learning; the antidote for aging is action, both mental and physical. For aging men and women it becomes increasingly important to transform old habits, get out of ruts, and avoid rigid ways. The human body can be compared to a car battery — keeping it running charges it. We can charge the battery by having the car run idly in the driveway or we can drive the car to an interesting and beautiful place that we really want to see.

And so, we seem to need to keep our bodies and minds active, not merely just doing something to keep busy but doing something that really interests us, something we've always wanted to do. It doesn't seem to matter what it is that we work at learning — it can be journal keeping, gourmet cooking, carpentry, a new language. It is the process of being actively involved in something of interest that is important. I'm saving up a few projects for my retirement years. I learned to speak German as a child, but I never actually studied the language. I'd like to become proficient in the mother tongue of my ancestors. I'd like to learn to play the piano. I want to learn to do these things because I want to, not just to fill empty hours.

Many older persons seem also to want to continue learning, considering the boom in adult education throughout our country. There are evening courses in our schools, which teach all kinds of new skills. The youngsters go to school during the day, the oldsters go to school at night — it's a nice image. Colleges and universities often permit older people to register for courses at a reduced rate, and so we have a mix of youngsters and oldsters learning side by side, exchanging rich experiences. There is a seriousness of purpose among those older people — they are there to learn. Educators have long espoused that education is a lifelong process. Our society seems to be coming more enlightened in this area.

We in education have learned slowly about the vast number of older persons who wish to return to school. In other areas of consumer marketing, older people have also been largely neglected. Their buying power is slowly being recognized. There are millions of Americans over 55; yet, it is as if these vast numbers of the aging do not exist. It seems that the young can't conceive what it is to be an older person and the resultant misconceptions are numerous.

One of the most devastating myths about older persons is that they suffer from some horrible disease — something worse than AIDS. Aging is a glorious accomplishment; it is the result of trial by fire, strength and survivorship. There is the debilitating assumption that older persons are powerless. The old are far from powerless; they are in fact emerging as one of the most influential voting blocs in America. The politician who ignores the older American does so at his own peril. Finally, there is the unfortunate misconception that older Americans are useless.

Older persons have so much to offer in wisdom, gleaned from their work and life experiences. They have mastered skills that are important for us to learn from them. There are many wonderful contributions they can make as consultants to business, education, and politics: as surrogate grandparents; as contributors to the art world through music, sculpture, painting; as people to learn from through every day interactions. When we regard the elderly as unattractive, obsolete, dull, and useless, we are painting portraits of our own future.

The foregoing assessment of old age is learned at a very young age. My grandson Clay, at four, asked me why Leslie's fourteen-year-old Golden Retriever couldn't walk up the stairs. "Why can't she?" he asked. I told him that Brandy was too old. He retorted, "Pa is 70, and he goes up the stairs pretty good." Then we had a discussion about animals' aging faster and not living as long as people. I find that children who care for and love animals have a greater understanding of life and death issues, which then may be built upon to appreciate the human life cycle.

One night, the famous writer Garson Kanin was listening to a TV editorial in favor of forced retirement. He became furious, demanded equal TV time, and got it. Here's what he said and wrote (1978)

> I'm Garson Kanin of New York, replying as a private citizen to a recent editorial which closed by saying, 'As a practical matter, we think mandatory retirement does make sense if the age chosen is a reasonable one.' Nonsense! Working men and women should retire for two reasons only: if they want to retire, or if they are unable to function. These conditions may occur at age 42 or 26 or 38 or 87. Setting a precise age is folly. We are all — thank God and nature different. I know many young people in their seventies — a few old fogies at forty. As a man condemned to death reckons his remaining days, he is conditioned. Four more — three more — two more — one — and he's ready for it. A man who is told on his sixty-fifth birthday he will no longer be useful, lives through the same sort of agonizing countdown — and finally allows a silly system to transform him overnight into a superfluous nonentity. What's the difference between killing a man and not allowing him to live? Of all the dangerous, destructive isms that have plagued this century, ageism is the most stupid. It's time to declare war on the mindless youth cult that has our time in its grip: demoralizing our people, weakening our system, depleting our energy, feeding our depression, wasting our experience, betraying our democracy, and blowing out our brains.

We begin sowing the seeds for what we will become at the beginning. We absorb the expectations of society, record the images of the elderly we encounter and those with whom we live. We gradually live into those images as a kind of self-fulfilling prophecy, so it becomes increasingly important for us to pay attention to the models of that which we wish to become.

We reap the harvest of old age from the seeds we are now sowing. We nurture, tend, and cultivate the fruits of our growing selves. If we do it well, life comes full circle, ultimately producing the vigorous seeds we leave as our heritage for the young.

If we live our lives fully and well, the issue of self-esteem will fade as a resolved issue in our older years and will become just one thread in the fabric of one's whole life. And this reality gives today its real importance. Today is all we have. How we use today is our best preparation for growing older.

CHAPTER IX

GIVING YOURSELF A HEARING

HUMAN BEINGS ARE FASCINATINGLY COMPLEX! Frequently it is easier to be friendly toward people we don't like than it is to be loving toward those for whom we care deeply. We can say what we are against, but often have difficulty in articulating what we are for. It seems easier to talk about what we do than it is to say who we are. And, it seems infinitely more difficult to learn to love and value ourselves than it is to dislike and discount ourselves.

The value we place upon ourselves is the most crucially important factor in our lives; it permeates and influences every facet of living. Self-esteem is the word we use to describe that feeling of worthiness. I don't like the word *self-esteem*; it sounds stiff and clinical to my ear; yet, it is the term most easily recognized when we discuss the valuing of self. Our level of self-esteem depends upon the extent to which we admire and value ourselves. Self-esteem is important; it affects everything we do. The irony is that we all seem to know this, but what to do to acquire self-esteem is the question.

Often we have a sense of hopelessness and helplessness when we look at our lives. We begin to ask: Who am I? How did I get here? Where am I going? What's it all about, anyhow? There is a sense of not being in control, of not having sufficient power. We feel overwhelmed, confused, and unable to identify the alternatives that exist for us. We give up and settle into narrow little ruts and won't risk the changes that are possible, if we had the courage to dare. But it needn't be that way. We have tremendous power. We can change our lives, become different people. We can learn to love, value, and esteem ourselves. We can do it ourselves, if we choose to do so.

A way to begin our search for self-esteem is to look at ourselves deeply and realistically. This is often a painful process. I know that I distort what I don't want to see, or like Scarlett O'Hara (*Gone With the Wind*) said, "I'll think about that tomorrow." At the same time, I'm storing data away in my head and in my journal. "I haven't said it to myself yet," is an expression I use when asked how I feel about something that I'm not ready to discuss. Saying it to myself is the signal that I am ready to become more actively involved. Once I begin saying it to myself, the connections and insights come very fast. I know a lot more than I think I know or admit to knowing!

As I write this, I have a flashback that makes me smile. As a young mother, I made many resolutions about rearing my first child, my son. One of my vows was to always answer his questions truthfully, painful though it might be. One day, when he was about seven, Allen asked me if there really was a Santa Claus. "No," I replied bluntly. "You and Dad buy all the presents, trim the tree?" "Yes," I said. Allen was quiet for a few moments and then said, "Well, I suppose there's no Easter Bunny and no good Tooth Fairy, either?" The insights and connections came quickly. He already had suspicions about Santa Claus or he would not have asked the question. Once he faced the loss of Santa, he was ready to give up the Easter Bunny and the Tooth Fairy. Awareness seems to lead to more awareness. However, he was not ready to rob his younger sister of her childhood innocence when he said to me, several years later, "If Leslie asks if there's a Santa Claus, tell her that there is."

I, too, go through life discovering that there is no Santa Claus — and then become aware there is no Easter Bunny or Tooth Fairy, either. Often I maintain a myth about relationships, about where I am in life, and what it is I want to do. I believe that I have a good and true friend only to discover that my confidences have been betrayed. When I pay attention to that hurt, when I say, "I have been betrayed," I open myself up to what really is. In the reflecting and healing process, I discover that, yes, it is true that I have been betrayed, that the friendship as I perceived it was only a fantasy on my part. Then I become aware that I have another friend who is always there when needed, who has never once let me down during these many years of friendship. I've taken that person for granted. If I had not felt the hurt of my perceived betrayal and explored it, I wouldn't have realized that I already had the kind of friendship for which I longed. Something new and better came into my life once I was able to explore the reality of pain.

We discover or become aware of what's happening in our lives by reflecting, thinking, and remembering. When we rely solely upon memory, we are dependent upon bits and pieces of hazy, partially remembered information. We become highly selective: don't remember certain things; do recall others. The data we recall may be inaccurate; then our perceptions become distorted. It's similar to looking at ourselves in a flawed mirror. The reflection looks like us, but it does not reflect the true image.

To collect more accurate information about our lives, we need to write it down. When data is written down, it is there, readily available for rereading and study. There is less chance of distorting or coloring that data, as often happens when we try to recall events and feelings. Once it is written down, we are free of trying to carry all that information in our heads. Often what seems unimportant, at the moment of writing, assumes greater importance when we try to make sense of feelings, thoughts, and perceptions. A tiny piece of forgotten information recorded may later be an important clue to a new discovery or an awareness about self.

A most productive device for recording the data of one's life is a journal. The widespread use of the journal as a tool for increasing personal awareness is a relatively recent phenomenon. Modern recognition of the relationship between the conscious and unconscious aspects of human behavior has led us to learn to use this device more effectively. We know that the unconscious is a vast resource of knowledge and information. Formerly, we relied heavily upon psychiatrists and psychologists to act as interpreters of this internal data. There seemed to be a mystique about the mind so we placed the psychological understanding of ourselves into the realm of the professionals. We didn't know that we were capable of exploring and understanding why we acted as we did. In a way, we abdicated responsibility for ourselves.

Mass media has helped to dispel much of this mystique. Developing increased self-awareness has become popular. It is becoming increasingly understood that this need not be a narcissistic, self-absorptive study, but, rather, the ability to step outside ourselves to see what's happening in our lives. The popular TV talk shows, such as *Oprah*, feature people who advise us how to interpret our dreams, how to overcome addictions, how to meditate, etc. We are further educated through the *Today Show*, *Good Morning America*, CNN, and radio talk shows. Popular magazines introduce us to many of these new concepts. Book stores and libraries have available material written for the novice as well as for the sophisticated reader. Information about personal growth is readily available and can be understood. Psychology is no longer a topic relegated to the textbook and lecture hall!

In the early 1960s, psychologist Ira Progoff created a journal to be used in working with the inner material of one's life. He believed that persons could discover resources within themselves they weren't even aware they possessed. His copyrighted *Intensive Journal* consists of a three-ring notebook with colored dividers. These provide sections for recording and working with the events in one's life, for dialoguing with persons, happenings, work, or anything else that requires attention. His method is highly structured but may be learned in the many workshops held throughout the United States. Progoff described his work as "a continuing confrontation with oneself in the midst of life," and as a psychological laboratory in which personal experience is recorded and studied to bring the outer and inner parts of one's experience into balance and harmony. His book, *At A Journal Workshop* (1975), describes this in detail.

Other sources which are helpful in the study of journal keeping as a tool for self growth are the writings of Anais Nin, Tristine Rainer, and May Sarton. Nin has described her own diary as a movement from "subjectivity and neurosis to objectivity, expansion, fulfillment." Rainer gives practical advice for dozens of productive ways to work with journal writing. Sarton reveals the personal agonies and joys she has encountered in her life and makes connections with her creative expression as a writer.

Several years ago, while writing my doctoral dissertation, I formulated the theory that keeping a journal would be instrumental in developing self-esteem. My theory was based upon the work of sociologists and psychologists, who had defined some elements of self-esteem, and upon the research of Sidney Jourard who suggested that there was a connection between self-disclosure and a healthy personality. Jourard (1964) wrote that he suspected he could not know his own soul or know his real self unless he disclosed himself to another. I found that when we are able to disclose ourselves to another person in personal interactions, we uncover our real self. As a client talks to his therapist, he reveals the data of his life. In the process of talking, the client begins to hear what he or she is saying. In effect, we give ourselves a hearing in the presence of another.

If disclosing self to another could be so beneficial, I reasoned, why was it not possible to reveal self to self? Instead of talking to a therapist or another person, I could talk to myself or give myself a hearing by writing in my journal. The journal becomes the other to whom I disclose myself. The journal reflects the image of self that I project. In the process of disclosing self to self, I believe that it is possible to become one's own "significant other." *Significant other* has been defined as the person to whom we tell our innermost secrets, the person to whom we look for affirmation, nurturance, and acceptance. We have seen that in order for persons to grow in healthy ways, it is essential that they receive loving recognition. It is my belief that we can give ourselves concerning, loving, and respectful treatment. We need to learn how to do that, how to teach ourselves that we are worthy of love. We need to unlearn that we are bad, unworthy of being loved. We must stop being embarrassed or shy about paying attention to ourselves.

I don't mean to suggest that we don't need other people in our lives — because, of course, we do. I do believe that we can become better architects of our lives and life styles if we pay attention to the process of living. It's the quality of the treatment we give to ourselves that is crucial to our well-being. Too often, we're not even aware of the way we do treat ourselves. The habits are so well ingrained and so familiar that we don't even think about many of the things we do to undermine self.

For instance, when was the last time that you did something nice for yourself — like buying a special treat, a garment you might have rejected because it cost too much? Sometimes I won't buy something for myself because it is too expensive — and then I'll purchase something much more expensive for one of my children without a second thought. Or, I'll stop at a fast food restaurant when I'm alone and gulp down a hamburger. I seldom do that when I'm with another. I'll buy paintings for gifts, but rarely buy an expensive one for myself. And I find myself running errands for loved ones when my energy is depleted and my time is limited. It's hard for me to say

"No," but I'm learning to do that without experiencing a tremendous guilt trip.

Again, it is not an either-or-situation. A balance must be struck. I'm not suggesting that we overextend our budgets or that we say "No" all of the time. We need to pamper ourselves, though, even in small ways. A friend ordered a double portion of bacon for breakfast the other morning, saying to the waitress, "I want it, and I deserve it." The bacon arrived on two separate plates, making the choice even more dramatic.

We should have a double order of bacon occasionally, if we feel like it. We can learn to take a leisurely bubble bath, as did the mother in an earlier chapter. Making these choices, which don't seem so very important on the surface, gets us into the habit of caring for ourselves. Taking care of ourselves in these ways helps prepare the way for working with more serious issues, such as, leaving a relationship which is no longer productive for one or both of the partners.

Terminating a relationship can be a traumatic experience. The one making the choice to leave often suffers as much as the one left behind. How do you tell someone who loves and cares for you deeply that you no longer wish to continue the relationship? You feel guilty, terrible for inflicting hurt. It must be done, though, in order to be real and true to one's self. Sometimes it is a relief to both partners when a relationship, no longer mutually productive, is terminated. Nevertheless, the pain of separation can be intense when it first happens.

Journal writing can be so helpful in situations like that. The one leaving is able to pour out feelings of guilt to that receptive ear, the journal. The one left who might be feeling rejected, abandoned, and betrayed can also pour those feelings onto the journal's pages. There is a tremendous unburdening when this is able to happen.

Rereading these pages later assists in the healing process, gives one a new perspective about life and increases awareness. We may be awed that the suffering was so acute and that the pain was endured and worked through. In rereading old journal pages, I'm able to finally forgive myself for something I've done. There is a wonderful feeling of freedom when that happens. I feel good about myself and my self-esteem soars.

This point is well illustrated by an entry in Anne Frank's diary (*The Diary of Anne Frank*). Kitty was the name Anne gave to her diary. Anne wrote in the beginning that she hoped Kitty (in effect, herself) would become her best friend:

Sunday 2 January, 1944

Dear Kitty,
  This morning when I had nothing to do I turned over some of the pages of my diary and several times I came across letters dealing with the subject of 'Mummy' in such a hot-headed way that I was quite shocked and asked myself, 'Anne, is it really you who mentioned hate. Oh, Anne, how could you!' I remained sitting with the open page in my hand and thought about it and how it came about that I should have been so brimful of rage and really so filled with such a thing as hate that I had to confide it all in you. I have been trying to understand the Anne of a year ago and to excuse her, because my conscience isn't clear as long as I leave with these accusations, without bothering to explain, in looking back, how it happened. I suffer now — and suffered then — from moods, which kept my head under water (so to speak) and only allowed me to see the things subjectively without enabling me to consider quietly the words of the other side, and to answer them as the words of one whom I, with my hot-headed temperament, had offended or made unhappy. I hid myself within myself. I only considered myself and quietly wrote down all my joys, sorrows and contempt in my diary. This diary is of great value to me, because it has become a book of memoirs in many places, but on a good many pages I could certainly put 'past and done with.'

That last phrase "past and done with" is such a powerful one. Problems had been worked with and resolved. In a way, Anne had forgiven herself for some of her feelings and negative thoughts. Diary entries helped her to study past events; she was shocked to find the extent of her feelings. Awareness developed from the rereading so she learned much about herself. This is the power of journal writing! Anne was able to give herself loving treatment through disclosure to her diary. She became her own significant other. She gave herself a hearing.

So much can be learned from rereading journal entries. With self-awareness, we are able to make better choices and to forge our own destiny. It is possible to get some clues from these entries and then to build upon them, developing strategies designed to improve our self-esteem, self image, and to help us feel more in control of our lives. There is so much power in this process! We take responsibility for ourselves, feel more in control of our destiny. For instance, we have learned that a factor in elevating self-esteem is a history of successes. Shouldn't it be possible for us to create some areas of success for ourselves, or perhaps to identify successes in our lives that we take for granted? Maybe we're great cooks, listen well, produce wonderful children, or create great gardens. It is so familiar that we don't realize there are many situations in which we do excel.

How one deals with anxiety is a component of self-esteem, so it becomes important to discover clues to what it is that makes us so anxious. We can find productive ways to reduce anxiety once we are aware of how we got to that place. Perhaps we become anxious when we anticipate meeting a person who in some way can influence our job. To prepare us for the real encounter — thinking about the meeting, rehearsing it, dialoguing with the person — we can learn to do through journaling.

The way a person responds to put-downs is another component in the development and maintenance of self-esteem. Do I collude in the put-downs? Do I evaluate my devaluation by another by focusing on that person's unresolved issues? Is the problem mine or his or hers? Are there toxic people in my life? People who make me not like myself in their presence? How do I deal with them? What role do I play in the process of devaluation? Who are the nurturing people in my life and how do I receive nourishment from them? Have I hugged my child today or told someone I value how much I care about them? How do I give nurturance to others? These are important questions. In order to answer them, we need information. Such data can be found in our journal.

How, then, does one go about keeping a journal? The word journal conjures up memories of that tiny volume from the dime store, with lined pages, dates for five years, and a small lock and key. The data which could be collected there was sparse; the amount of space also limited what could be written down and the avenues of creativity.

The choice of journal is important for some people, not so important for others. I have seen elaborately embossed leather journals and bound books with empty pages and silk-screen print covers. Many people use ledgers, composition books, and spiral leaf notebooks. The choice is individual; the person writing a journal should choose something comfortable. The point is to have empty pages, beckoning and inviting.

I have an aversion to lined paper; those tiny lines divert my mind, cramp my thinking, so I prefer an unlined journal. I have trouble with writing in a bound book; the rigid spine leads me to begin writing halfway across the page. I discovered that a loose-leaf notebook, which slips into a simple leather cover. works well for me. For some, this conjures up memories of school and homework. I like it, though; it seems appropriate for me and my style. Each person needs to make a choice which invites writing rather than one that shouts, "This is a chore!" Nor should the journal be so beautiful that the journaler chooses not to use it.

The wonderful thing about keeping a journal is that there is no right or wrong way to do it. No one is going to correct the grammar or spelling; no one will judge the quality of the writing except you, yourself. And so the way to begin is simply to begin. Buy your book, sit or lie down and begin writing whatever comes into your head. You may wish to write sitting next to a pond, on top of a mountain, at a desk, in the bathtub, or in bed. You can write in the early morning, late evening, or any time of the day that suits you. The important thing is to write; write when you feel like doing it. You needn't write every day; although, some people feel more comfortable with having a period of time allocated for journal writing. Find your own way; just begin!

Many people feel self-conscious when they first begin journal writing. Remember that you are writing for yourself so you don't have to make up things to make the reading more interesting. Honesty is what is needed. You will find quickly that your deepest thoughts and feelings are dramatic and fascinating. It is in the honesty, which flows onto the journal page, that you will find the clues to your real self. That is what you want. Nothing is too terrible, dull, or earth-shaking to tell your journal. If you ask "Am I really writing this?" you probably are working with some important material.

And, write quickly. Write about your relationships, fears, doubts, joys. Flow onto the page. How is life for you at this particular moment? What have you seen recently that touched you or gave you pain? What's happening in your life? Write down your dreams, your fantasies. Keep copies of letters — sent and unsent. Write a word portrait of yourself or loved ones. Include sketches, doodles. All of these represent glimpses of your life.

Sometimes I begin a journal entry by talking to myself. I call this process "Giving myself a hearing." The idea of talking to myself by writing it down is one that I find exciting and useful in my life. When I go beyond the state, "I don't know; I haven't said to myself yet," and focus my thinking through writing, then I'm stating the problem. The most productive way of saying something is to actually write it down in the journal.

I often talk to myself via my journal. When I listen to what I'm saying, become aware of what's happening in my inner world. If I'm feeling depressed, I talk to myself about it, trying to discover why. Sometimes I can do something about the situation – perhaps by changing the environment. Simply writing about a situation can serve to change it. Frequently I discover that I'm feeling anxious because I have said or done something thoughtless and rude to another. If I can write a note or make a telephone call saying that I'm sorry, or if I can simply explain what was happening in me in that moment, I almost always feel better, more peaceful.

It was from my journal that I learned that this was a useful way to work with my feelings. The entries show what I said, then I get a sense of uneasiness, and then comes the awareness that I had hurt someone. An example of this was an incident involving my daughter Lisa. She arranged her new bedroom furniture so proudly and enthusiastically; then "Come see my room, Mom!" I looked and said, "Why did you put all your junk in those drawers?" Lisa became quiet and said, "It's not junk, Mom. It's my books and papers." It was later that I became aware of the word junk — it fairly leaped from my journal page. How thoughtless and judgmental! I immediately sought out Lisa to say that I was sorry I had been so insensitive, that I had undermined her joy of the moment. She gave me a hug of understanding. Before journal keeping, I would have felt uneasy for several days, unable to put my finger on the cause of my disquietude. As soon as I had written in my journal that evening, I knew what I had done wrong. From writing down just such small examples I've learned that if I don't deal with such incidents right away, they have a way of mushrooming inside me and alienating relationships.

Joyful experiences recorded also give me insight into ways I can enrich my life. As I reread old journal entries, I discovered that the color of water gives me a great deal of pleasure. I love the greens of the Florida Keys' water — it has a quality of color I haven't seen anywhere else: not the deep blue of Curaco or the blue of Bermuda! Now when I plan a vacation, I usually ask myself, "What water color am I in the mood for?" This seems as important as climate or facilities. I wasn't really aware of that until I saw how often I commented upon water in my journal. Writing about joyful experiences is doubly rewarding: reading what I've written helps relive the moment.

Once upon a time in journal writing, I tended to write about what was troubling me so I soon had a volume of everything that was wrong in my life. I would become depressed upon rereading the entries. One day I said to myself, "Wait a minute, how about that glorious sunset you saw on that day when everything seemed to be going wrong? Just sitting in the car, watching that awesome panorama gave you a deep sense of peacefulness and helped melt away all those feelings of frustration, and you didn't even record it!"

Joy and happiness play important roles in my life, too, and I learned through the journal entries I chose to record that, in the past, I used to feel self-conscious about writing down loving, supportive comments made to me. I had no trouble recording the hurtful, sarcastic ones. I learned that when I focused upon the negative feelings in my life, I engaged in self-defeating behavior that lowered my self-esteem. Now I write about those love pats and strokes too, and it feels just as good at the second and third reading as it did when initially received. I also staple letters and notes I receive in my journal. I used to keep what I called a treasure box in which I placed those precious, meaningful mementos of my life. Now they go into my journal, no longer sealed in a separate vault, but right there in the full flow of my life.

Not only did I initially have a problem with recording positive anecdotes about myself and of filing away positive feedback, but I also had a problem dealing with anger. I learned as a child that young girls don't get angry or have temper tantrums, that the terrible consequence of displaying anger was to have people not like you. I remember my brother teasing me; nothing I said or did made him stop so, in frustration, I picked up a bowl of mashed potatoes and threw it at him. My brother didn't speak to me for a month. It was as if I didn't exist. I can still recall the terrible, heavy feeling I had and the guilt I carried as a result of that act. I learned to control my temper, as admonished by my mother and by my brother's silence. The learning consisted of denying my feelings; although, I often cried instead, giving vent to my emotions in a more acceptable and ladylike way, more acceptable than screaming or throwing things! However, keeping my head in the sand is a familiar condition. I often want things to go the way I want them to be, and so part of me pretends that it is so. Another part of me knows full well about the pretense and busily stores away data more descriptive of reality.

Writing in my journal helps me to cope with anger in a way that is more acceptable to me than crying, for instance. I usually begin an entry with, "I am so angry!" and then say exactly why I am angry, describe the circumstances surrounding the event provoking the emotion, which soon leads me to understand why I am experiencing that feeling. So very often, I discover that the event has triggered an old, forgotten, and unresolved experience so that the anger of the moment has more to do with a memory from the past — when I felt powerless — than it does with the happening of the moment. Sometimes I discover that my anger is justified and requires further action. I am now able to pick up the telephone or to encounter a person directly and say, "I am angry with you," and state the reason. Not only is this honest expression healthy for me, it is often appreciated by the other person. Instead of being cool and remote, I verbalize my truth, and the air can be cleared. I'm not able to do that all the time, of course, but the more able I am to be honest, the better I feel about myself and the other. Writing an unsent letter is often a way I express anger or other emotions. If for some reason I don't want to encounter another person directly, writing down my feelings releases or vents the emotion, and relieves the burden I feel inside. There are many letters I'm glad I haven't sent; keeping them in my journal provides another source of data to study and to learn.

I have discovered that much of my anger comes from a sense of impotence, a feeling of being out of touch with my own power. It's related to the deep need to be liked and appreciated by others. That need diminishes as I am more able to like and appreciate myself. When I voice my feelings, I am acknowledging that I have a right to be a person with normal feelings, that I don't have to be superwoman, trying to project the image of perfection. When I verbalize my dissatisfaction with others' behavior, I'm also saying to the other that there are certain behaviors which are unacceptable to me. All this is related to feelings of self-esteem.

A problem I'm currently working on is an illness – asthma. While I've not had any serious illnesses, the recurring bouts of asthma are frightening. Four times in one year I went to the hospital's emergency room to receive adrenaline and other injections. The results are dramatic — one moment I'm gasping for breath and feel as if I'm dying and fifteen minutes later, after I receive medication, my breathing becomes normal. An hour later I leave the hospital feeling well and relaxed.

My doctor says asthma is a disease and that I must accept it. Acceptance is the first step in controlling any chronic illness. I hate all the medication and tend to take it only when having an acute attack, even though I know the medicine is intended to prevent rather than cure. I want to be cured; I don't want a lifetime of various medicines every four hours to prevent attacks. I say the medication has a terrible odor and taste; the doctor says no one else has ever complained. I call my sister, a nurse, to tell her about my illness. She says I should be happy that I don't have diabetes which often requires the amputation of a limb. It doesn't comfort me!

I had a dialogue with my asthma to see what I could learn. The dialoguing process is a useful exercise to bring to awareness the possible cause of a particular problem. I know that emotional and psychological factors contribute to an illness as well as environmental and biological factors. In the dialoguing, I actually talked to the asthma and had it talk back to me:

ME: I'm so angry with you! You're disrupting my life. I'm losing sleep. I'm feeling anxious. I hate you. You make me feel weak and dependent.

ASTHMA: I make you feel weak and dependent? How did I come into your life anyhow? You were told ten years ago you had allergies and that you had to avoid dust, feathers, spices, and numerous other things. You laughed! 'Impossible,' you said, when the allergist told you to remove your carpeting and drapery. How could a little cinnamon bother you? Live without wine? 'Forget it!' you said. And, you did. So, don't blame me for your self-defeating behavior.

ME: Yes, I have to admit that's true. I wouldn't even say the word asthma — I'd say I had a few allergies, easily controlled by Dristan. But then the Dristan didn't work.

ASTHMA: Do you remember the first attack you had? For days you denied that you were ill. You had to sleep sitting up. You couldn't breathe properly. 'It's only the pollen from the plant,' you said, even though it was February. 'Maybe it's the candle.' When you finally gave in and went to the hospital, you were shocked when they asked you how long you'd had asthma. 'Who me?' you said, 'I only have allergies.' You wouldn't stay there either when the doctor wanted you to check in as a patient.

And so the dialogue went. In the process I discovered that I had been denying and had to take responsibility for an illness which I had refused to acknowledge. I also discovered that almost every attack had been preceded by a stressful incident. So I learned that anger turned inward helped precipitate an asthma attack. I felt choked up emotionally and then became choked up physically. It seems clear that emotional factors do influence our physical condition. When in the midst of an attack, anxiety increases the security, further closing down the tubes. A session with a medical doctor, who also teaches self-hypnosis, was most helpful to me. He made a tape, using imagery promoting peacefulness, which I use to relax and control my breathing. I play the tape every day; it has become a very important part of my life. While the asthma problem is far from solved, I am working on it and I can manage it. Perhaps one day, like Anne Frank, I'll be able to say, "past and done with." I believe there is much yet to be learned about asthma; there are clues buried in my journal which need to be surfaced to further understand this illness.

I discovered, through journaling, that problems become more stressful when we feel powerless to do something about them. Simply writing them down provides a wonderful relief, even before we actively try to solve them. It's as if we're already taking action by acknowledging that we have a problem when we record it, so journaling is a start-up process.

There is no special magic or formula that can be given for working through personal problems with journal material. Situations vary; each person is unique. What works for me is giving complete expression to the problem by free flowing writing. There is a catharsis in letting thoughts and feelings flow onto the page of a journal. Perhaps some of the writing appears childish and immature as it is reread, but insights and perspectives about life are gained in a mature way. Acknowledging problems and working with them frees psychic energy. There is a tremendous sense of unburdening.

One does not need a tremendous amount of information in order to begin the process of journal keeping. The way to begin, as I've said, is to begin writing. In the writing, we begin to discover that it is possible to give ourselves loving and concerned attention. Feelings of personal worth, confidence, and adequacy are not lofty goals beyond our reach. We learn and acquire these attitudes just as we learn to feel unworthy and inadequate. Debilitating feelings may be unlearned as acquired new feelings take their place. It's not easy, but it is possible.

All of us have so much potential. We can learn to use it more productively, to enrich our own lives and the lives of those we touch. It is so sad to look about us and to see all the wasted, untapped potential, to observe the number of persons who have settled for meager existences, never knowing the joy of loving and appreciating themselves and others. For we can never truly learn to love another until we learn to love ourselves.

When healthy people feel that they are persons of dignity and worth, they behave in that way. They see themselves as likable, acceptable, able, and worthy. Happy and self-accepting people are more able to accept others.

How sad that our focus has been upon what's wrong with us! How easily we are able to tell valued others in our lives what's wrong with them, often expecting them to know automatically that we love and cherish them. How hard and unforgiving we are toward ourselves! Just imagine if we could manage to produce one generation of persons who were all taught from the very beginning that they are worthy of love and compassion! Imagine if they could be taught to deeply love themselves! Our world truly would be a kinder and gentler place.

To achieve the good life, Socrates said, "Know thyself." Knowing oneself deeply and fully is not an easy task. It often means facing oneself squarely and honestly. It means learning to forgive ourselves and others. It means making peace with ourselves and reconciling in a realistic way the discrepancies between our hopes and dreams and our actual accomplishments. It means accepting in some deep way that a real self is someone that we create and nurture.

CHAPTER X

AND SO?

I HAVE SPENT YEARS writing this book. In a way, the writing has been therapeutic; it has been a public kind of journal. My deepest and darkest secret has been illuminated; it has been researched, probed, and examined from every conceivable angle. The secret is no longer a secret — I had difficulty in esteeming myself. I had trouble with seeing myself as a worthy human being.

A strange thing happened during the writing of this book — the more I wrote the better I began to feel about myself. I began writing in the second person and then changed you to I as I reread my work. As I tried to tell you about self-esteem, I realized I was talking to me. As I struggled to teach you about self-esteem, I learned it for myself.

I am a first generation American and, if my parents had not come to the United States, I would be a very different person. I carry within me the memory of European culture. European cuisine is like mother's milk to me; my love foods are the ones my mother cooked and served to me. She learned those recipes from her mother, and I have handed them down to my children.

German pancakes, pfanskuchen, are a special treat, soothing the psyche as well as the palate. They conjure up memories of my mother standing at the coal stove making them in her old black frying pan. Now I stand at my electric range, using that same pan, to make those same pancakes. Not only do they represent a love food to my children but to my brother as well. Recently I visited him in Arizona, and I made some for him. He ate 12, pronouncing them to be "Just like Mom's!" The making and eating of those pancakes was more than an exercise in cooking and eating, it was reliving and passing on the love expressed to us by our mother. Someday, perhaps, my daughters will visit their brother and make pancakes for him, "Just like Mom made." Knowing my son, though, he could make his own pfanskucken!

There are many such examples in my life: lessons learned from ancestors, folklore that has me thinking and feeling what I think they felt and appreciated. As I sit here writing in the present moment, my mind drifts back to the past and then to dreams about the future. The present moment is an interlude between the past and the future. For me to live fully in this moment, I've found it necessary to relive some of the moments of the past. I became curious about how I came to be the person I am. Most of all, I wanted to discover why I had such a problem with self-esteem. Thus began my lifelong study.

There are many definitions of self-esteem. Some advocates of self-esteem have an understanding of the multifaceted states of self-esteem. Critics seem only to have a knowledge of what self-esteem basically is not. Branden (1994) speaks to the current general understanding of self-esteem:

> The question is sometimes asked, "Is it possible to have too much self-esteem?" No, it is not; no more than it is possible to have too much physical health or too powerful an immune system. Sometimes self-esteem is confused with boasting or bragging or arrogance; but such Traits reflect not too much self-esteem, but too little; they reflect a lack of self-esteem (p. 19).

Contrast Branden's statement with Talbot's (2002): "Last year alone there were three withering studies of self-esteem released in the United States, all of which had the same central message: people with high self-esteem pose a greater threat to those around them than people with low self-esteem and feeling bad about yourself is not the cause of our country's biggest, most expensive social problem" (p. 44). My understanding and lived experience of self-esteem is more in accord with Branden's definition.

In her article, Talbot reports that now over 2,000 how-to books have been published on the topic. When I began research on self-esteem for a doctoral dissertation in the late 1960s, there was little or no reference to the term self-esteem in the literature or in psychology. Two definitions of self-esteem were offered at that time: One by William James (1890) and another by Stanley Coopersmith (1967), which I utilized for my study. James had a formula, which was not very helpful to my study:

$$\text{Self-esteem} = \frac{\text{Success}}{\text{Pretensions}}$$

Coopersmith's definition and work became the core of my study. His book, *The Antecedents of Self-Esteem*, is still considered one of the best on the subject. His definition of self-esteem is:

> By self-esteem we refer to the evaluation that the individual makes and customarily maintains with regard to himself: it expresses an attitude of approval or disapproval, and indicates the extent to which the individual believes himself to be capable, significant, successful, and worthy. In short, self-esteem is a personal judgment of worthiness that is expressed in the attitudes the individual holds toward himself.

My self-esteem definition is a simple one: *self-esteem is the value we place upon inner selves.* There seems to be an unwritten law or adage that any part of one's life not fully experienced at the time needs to be lived though and resolved at a later period in life. My friend who married his first girlfriend at age twenty felt the need to terminate his marriage at forty. He says he felt as if he had never experienced young adulthood, never had a chance "to sow wild oats." Now he wants to experience new and different relationships. From my self-esteem perspective, his values are concentrated outside himself when he thinks a new relationship will enhance his self-image. An image of self is not a real self. He is doomed to repeat his past performances unless he works on his inner self to gain positive self-esteem.

I was seemingly unaffected by the death of my father fifty years ago, but recently I became overwhelmed by the death of a friend. I was pregnant when my father died and was told I had to be careful not to injure my child. So I didn't acknowledge the grief, didn't shed a tear. When my friend died, I seemed to experience the grief out of all proportion. I got in touch with my feelings of pain over the loss of my father. I realized that because I kept seeing him in his coffin as I looked at my dead friend, I felt better when, at last, I was able to cry and to mourn. Somehow I feel lighter and more complete now that my grieving for my father is "past and done with."

When I was eight-years-old, I remember "staying in" at recess on numerous occasions with my sister because she hadn't done her homework. She was two years younger than I, yet we were in the same classroom of our little country school. The teacher's rationale was that since I was older, I should make my sister do her work! I still remember my feelings of hopelessness, anger, and injustice. When I explored those days more fully, I became aware that the teacher wanted my sister to learn, but she probably didn't realize that she was punishing me. Once I relived my anger, I understood why I had such a dislike of that teacher, why she behaved as she did, why I tried harder to be affirming and understanding of my three children's learning experiences, and why I became the kind of teacher I did.

To get to the truth of our feelings, we need to discover who we were, what choices we made, what decisions we reached. Focusing upon how we felt and the choices we made seems to be essential for self-understanding. Rather than blame others in our lives, we take responsibility for ourselves when we seek to understand who and what we were at each phase. There is a profound difference in blaming others for our condition, and wallowing in self-pity, and taking responsibility for changing our lives for the better.

When we open and recycle the past, we can often correct childhood memories and discover new insights as adults that we can put into action. Limited or incorrect information and a child's point of view tend to lead to misconceptions. A woman I know, whose mother died of cancer when she was a young child, carried feelings of guilt and responsibility. Once she was able to relive those years, it became very clear to her that she was not responsible for her mother's death. So obvious! Unfortunately, those erroneous beliefs form in our childish minds; then they take root, flourish, and grow, bearing bitter fruit in our adult years! It is never too late to free ourselves from our past and to heal our wounds.

To move on with life, it is important to relive or explore past moments. There is a catharsis in attempting to understand who and why we are as we are. Burdens carried, knowingly and unknowingly, become lighter or disappear when we are willing to look at our behavior which represents them. Those unopened packages pushed back into the dark corners of our minds need to be opened, examined, aired, and acted upon. Too often we're afraid to open those closed packages, fearing we will find out some awful or unbearable secret about ourselves. So then we carry them, not quite forgetting but not quite remembering them either, setting up a vague, nagging, tugging of something unfinished in our lives. An emotional release comes from remembering and exploring. It seems necessary to stay with the pain of memories, if there are any, in order to have a complete catharsis. If we feel guilt and self-pity, it's a signal that we must go deeper, remember more, and be more honest with ourselves. Once we get past the initial pain of a particular memory, there is joy in at last being able to understand. That's how it was for me.

I have a young friend who has a doll she calls Callie. She tells me that when she is troubled or upset, she "packages" those troubles, holds Callie, and then "gives" her the packages. She feels "free," she says, after that little ritual.

Our minds are strangely or happily — however you choose to look at it — adept at not fully remembering or instant recall. How nice it would be to push a button and have the memory tapes immediately available. Instead, we have to dig and prod to find out things about ourselves and why we behave the way we do. Sometimes we can confront the past directly, but most times we have to sneak the information out of ourselves.

How can we arrive at a better understanding of ourselves? When we look at others, we seem to see them with perfect vision. We see their weaknesses, their flaws, and their goodness. With ourselves we often choose tunnel vision, seeing only the distortions, self-deceptions, refusing to acknowledge our goodness and strengths. We can learn about ourselves by observing others, but I believe it is essential to probe within self to know self. The task is to learn where and how to probe. The magic lies in learning to step outside ourselves to observe — almost as if we were looking at another person. It's hard to look into a mirror and really see ourselves. No mirror ever reflects our true image. If we can learn to look at the reflected image, observing the pleasant features, noting the flaws, we can learn much about ourselves.

With our physical reflection there is the possibility of cosmetic surgery, if we are not pleased with some of our features. We can also learn to enhance our good features, to play down the ones that are not so pleasing to us or to others. Skillful makeup detracts from a large nose, calls attention to beautiful eyes. Some of us, however, learn to live proudly with our features "as is." I am reminded of Barbara Streisand's nose. She has learned to emphasize it, draw attention to it. Her face has become one-of-a-kind. It is her hallmark. Rather than change her face, she has capitalized upon it.

Our psychological selves can be changed too. Perhaps there is a part of that psychological self that we keep buried, and refuse to acknowledge, simply because we are ashamed of it, think it is ugly, or are afraid to use it. Perhaps it is a quality that society has not found attractive or desirable so we won't allow it to be presented to the world. I think of our cultural taboos for men and women. Most men kept their tenderness and soft side well hidden for fear of being perceived as weak. Today it is not unusual to see men's tears or to hear them express their vulnerability. Most women, too, have learned to acknowledge traits that were formerly thought of as masculine, such as assertiveness, aggressiveness, and independence. Rather than present ourselves as helpless, clinging vines, many of us have learned to say, "This is who I am. I am capable, competent, and feminine."

Whether we realize it or not, we all carry a mental image of self, although it may be blurred and distorted and hidden deeply within. The image is there, though, complete to the last minute detail. It has been developed from our beliefs about ourselves. Many of those beliefs were formed from past experiences: our successes, failures, humiliations, joys, and triumphs. We have learned, in previous chapters, how others have impacted upon us, helping us define that blueprint of self. Once the belief about ourselves goes into that picture, it seems forever etched. We don't stop to question the validity of our beliefs; we act as if they were true. All of our feelings, actions, and behavior become consistent with this image. We remain true to the picture we have of ourselves. From it we draw feelings of value and worth. Our judgment of our self's worth is called self-esteem.

We act like the person we perceive ourselves to be. The man who sees himself as a failure finds some way to fail and continues to maintain a negative level of self-esteem. He applies for a job even though he is inwardly convinced that he won't get it. He projects anxiety, insecurity, and feels that he really doesn't have the qualities the employer is seeking. It's no surprise when he really is rejected. He would be astounded to learn he invited that rejection by his hang-dog manner and altered his destiny:

Is our destiny in our self-concept?

> ...it tends to be. Our self-concept is who and what we consciously and subconsciously think we are--our physical and psychological traits, our assets and liabilities, possibilities and limitations, strengths and weaknesses. A self-concept contains or includes our level of self-esteem, but is more global. We cannot understand a person's behavior without understanding the self-concept behind it (Branden, 1994, p. 15).

Self-image can be changed. Self-esteem can be elevated. It is never too late for us to begin to change, to begin to live new lives. The secret of a productive, happy life is wholesome, healthy self-esteem. We must have a self to trust and to believe in, a self that is acceptable to us, a self we don't need to hide or cover up.

When our self-esteem is intact and secure, we feel good. When it is threatened, we feel anxious and insecure. It seldom occurs to us that these feelings evolve from our own evaluation of ourselves, and it is desirable to dynamically balance feelings with cognitive realities.

Learning who we are and becoming more means accepting our basic strengths and limitations while, at the same time, struggling to fulfill our potential. On the one hand, we say we need to love and accept ourselves as we are. On the other hand, we must learn to change ourselves, to open up new possibilities in order to fulfill our promise. There is an ongoing tension between these two concepts when we try to live productive and creative lives. A healthy kind of self-acceptance emphasizes the best that is within us. It tries to change what we can, accept what we cannot.

A healthy approach to dissatisfaction could be aimed at those areas of thinking, behaving, and feeling that interfere with our potential to become what we could be. How nice it would be to have a built-in control panel to flash red lights when we do something not in keeping with developing our full potential!

My car has negative indicators on the dashboard which flash red when there is something wrong — when the gas tank is nearly empty, when the oil pressure is too low, when the engine is becoming overheated. As I drive, I look at these indicators and make a mental note that all is well. When one of them flashes red, I look for the nearest service station to tend to the car's needs. I don't think about disposing of my car when a red light flashes; rather, I sensibly choose to remedy the situation immediately.

I am not so attentive to my own needs, though. Frequently I don't even acknowledge the inner red lights flashing that tell me I'm feeling anxious, full of stress until I become deeply dissatisfied with myself. Then I wish I could trade myself in for a new model. I see everything wrong with myself — all my weaknesses and incapabilities. When we focus on everything wrong with us, we don't see anything that's right about us.

We don't do that with our cars. We look through the windshield, focus on the road, concentrate upon where we're going, only occasionally glancing at the control panel. If we kept our eyes on the negative indicators exclusively, we'd soon be steering toward trouble for we'd soon lose sight of the road we're traveling.

Self-acceptance is a complex issue. When we lack self-approval, it usually means we have not yet developed a self-concept we believe is true. Then we seek approval from others, asking them to tell us we are OK. This usually means we substitute the opinions of others for self's approval.

Looking for approval from others in order to define ourselves, to tell us who and what we are and what we are not, can be self-defeating. When we present ourselves in ways designed to demand others' attention, respect, and good will, it takes considerable energy. We continually have to remember the role we've presented; often the presentation varies from person to person, taking on nuances of difference. It becomes so complex, so taxing to remember that to John we must present ourselves as a clinging vine to gain his approval and to Joe we need to appear aggressive and assertive to gain his acceptance. Some day we might forget and reveal the assertive self to John and the dependent one to Joe!

In the process of playing these various roles, we distance ourselves from the real self. We really know inside that any undeserved accolades received from a well-played role ensues from a false presentation of ourselves. We know within ourselves when we say things without meaning them and when we offer friendship without intending commitment. We know when we smile empty smiles and offer helping hands with no intention of a follow-up. Ultimately we can believe what others say about us only when we believe that others see us as we really are.

The behavior connected to genuine self-acceptance comes from a different place. Instead of trying to win approval through deception, we seek understanding and acceptance through honest self-disclosure, to ourselves as well as to others. People who achieve a high level of self-esteem don't seem to be paralyzed by the fear of failing; they are free to explore their capabilities, to test their limits, and to develop their untapped potential. In fact, self-esteem seems to come most forcefully to those who have the courage to investigate their areas of deepest self-doubt and to change.

Self-alienation is the other side of self-acceptance. When we fail to acknowledge or accept certain aspects of self, alienation results. Those unaccepted aspects are then perceived to be foreign. Although we tend to rationalize about our disowned capacities, they do not cease to exist. Often we project those characteristics onto another person, so we can view other people with indignation. We tend to hate in others those things which we despise in ourselves. The woman who acts strong and self-sufficient, while denying her occasional need to be taken care of, may feel a strong loathing for the woman who can be dependent, when necessary. The person who longs to experiment with his sexuality may label as promiscuous those who engage in different modes of sexual expression. By despising people like that, he affirms his belief that he is above that sort of behavior. When we begin to protest too much about others, we might well ask ourselves the question, "What is there about this person which reminds me of something in myself that I don't like?" Self-acceptance is a crucial step in maintaining a healthy self-image and in developing self-esteem. If we do not feel as adequate as other human beings, what then?

It is important for us to understand that a sense of inferiority is learned; it is not something with which we are born. Thus, this condition can be unlearned. Inferiority feelings are the result of many frustrations and experiences of failure. In addition, we begin to feel inferior as a result of being told by others that we are inferior. We have seen in previous chapters how the way we are treated by others — particularly authority figures — impacts upon our feelings of worthiness.

Feelings of inferiority do not always reflect the actual truth or condition. A beautiful woman may suffer from feelings of inferiority. The president of a prestigious company, the top-ranking student, the gifted athlete — all may be the subject of envy — but still feel inferior. The plain woman, an employee of an ordinary company, the poor student and mediocre athlete may not feel inferior at all. How we feel about those things and what we aspire to be make all the difference. Feelings of inferiority result when there is a wide discrepancy between our perceptions of ourselves and of our aspirations or the way we'd like to be. When we compare ourselves unfavorably with others, even if it is on an unconscious level, there is a felt sense of inadequacy.

If those feelings are not changed to positive ones, deeply rooted attitudes of inferiority leading to negative self-esteem take hold of us. Many of us are not even aware of the symptoms of inferiority and negative self-esteem in ourselves or in those whose lives we touch. How can we recognize the symptoms? What are the flashing signals which should warn us, and, once we recognize them, what can we do about them? Many psychologists have outlined the symptoms of inferiority and negative self-esteem. The following are a few I've gleaned from them and from my own understanding of self-esteem: self-hatred, acting as a loner, easily persuaded; they also include feelings of paranoia and the inability to accept criticism.

Once an area of negative self-esteem has been identified and acknowledged, it can be worked with to increase self-awareness. Sometimes a perceived negative quality cannot be erased; however, other assets can be developed to detract or offset the handicap. Eleanor Roosevelt, a shy, awkward, unattractive woman by society's standards, became an honored and revered leader. She began by being the eyes, ears, and legs for her paralyzed husband, Franklin D. Roosevelt, and emerged as a responsible, compassionate woman in her own right. When we think of her, we remember a woman, beautiful in spirit, who made a profound impact upon the entire world.

When we achieve in one area of our lives, a sense of worthiness is experienced and compensates for not doing so well in other areas. The man with marital problems may find peace and happiness in his children or in his job. A woman with a boring job may find satisfaction in a theatre group. An alcoholic may learn to build bars rather than to sit at one. Hobbies and sports are the mainstays of the majority of Americans. It is vital that we have something in our lives to give us satisfaction and pleasure.

Personal values we cherish also serve to enhance positive self-esteem. What is it that we value in our lives? We seem to esteem the qualities that support the way we see ourselves, the way we like to behave. When we regard good looks as being important, and we are good-looking, then it does not concern us if we have no mechanical ability since that is not a personal value. If we value good grades and do not value being physically attractive, then it is not so crucial to be attractive. If we value good grades and good looks, then there will be a conflict if we don't have both. The selection of personal values and acting upon them are related to self-esteem.

The achievement of a goal is important, not the kind of goal we set. The young man who aspires to be a builder can be as self-satisfied as the young man who aspires to be a lawyer and becomes one. The choosing of a goal, and then achieving it, leads to a feeling of satisfaction and worthiness. The person who aspires to become a teacher and fails did not achieve the goal; therefore, his self-esteem suffers a blow. Often it seems, we do select goals that are within the realm of our capabilities. It is unusual to set a goal that we feel is beyond our abilities. Somehow, we seem to assess our talents and focus upon what we want to be and make it happen. Problems arise when parents or other authority figures choose our goals for us or when we choose career goals for reasons other than to fulfill our passion. Not all of us aspire to be a matinee idol or President of the United States. I think of my son Allen telling me, when he was five-years-old, that he didn't think he could become President of the United States, but he thought he could be elected governor of New Jersey. He did neither, but became vice-president of a large investment firm, earning a salary larger than both. Even at that age, he was setting goals that he felt he could attain.

The quest for social acceptance is a major task affecting all of us. We seem to seek out the company of people who like us, with whom we agree and share similar beliefs and values, which enhances our self-worth and self-esteem. We rarely seek out or cultivate others who disagree with us or are critical. Hence, we have a mutual admiration group. Even top executives bring their own "men" with them when they change jobs. If we interact only with the people who never challenge us and always agree with us, we are rarely in the position to rethink our ideas and opinions, including of ourselves. The best kind of friend might be the one who gives us honest but caring feedback, challenging our beliefs without threatening us with the possibility of rejection if we don't agree. We do ourselves a disservice if we surround ourselves with "yes" people, usually stunting our ability to grow.

This seems to be such a very important kind of life tension. We need to be loved, nurtured, and affirmed in order to have healthy positive regard for ourselves. By the same token, we need to be challenged occasionally in order to grow and change. If we associate only with the people who are like us, we never learn another point of view. If we associate only with people who put us down, our self-esteem suffers. Again, it is the balance that is so important — having people and situations that nurture us and having people and situations that stretch us, help us to grow.

Some of us see ourselves as being extremely worthy; some of us see ourselves as being worthless. How does that happen? A contributing factor in self-esteem development is the influence of parents and other authority figures in our formative years. While we are free to choose our friends, we were not able to choose our parents, teachers, or classmates. When our parents reject us, teachers belittle us, or classmates jeer at us, there is little we can do to avoid their company and criticism. As children we are a captive audience and must participate day after day after day in the process which molds and shapes our personalities and future.

As children, we must abide by our parents' rules. These rules are their choices, not ours. We must do as they say. The selections parents make for us put a limitation on the options we have and become powerful influences on our self-esteem. The neighborhood that parents choose to live in dictates the kind of playmates we will have, the kind of school we will attend. If we are rejected or disparaged, we may feel unworthy and insignificant. Early in life, we perceive reflections of how others see and experience us.

Once again, we see the powerful impact that childhood experiences can have on our adult feelings. If we have been loved and nurtured, chances are we feel good about ourselves. If we have been unloved and rejected, we tend to feel that there is something wrong with us, that we are unworthy of being loved. How can we love ourselves when the message transmitted has been that we are "damaged goods?" A parent, teacher, adult, or child who transmits that message to unique, developing human beings is guilty of treason and should be publicly exposed and reprogrammed, for society is being deprived of its future responsible citizens.

It is well-known in our society that "Just as there are dysfunctional families, there are dysfunctional schools and dysfunctional organizations. They are dysfunctional because they place obstacles in the path of the appropriate exercise of mind" (Branden, 1994, p. 62), body, emotions, and spirit. Developmental obstacles hinder the growth necessary to become fully functioning human beings who are needed to perpetuate a democratic society; then all have an opportunity to flourish.

There is little doubt that our mental well-being depends deeply upon our feelings and thoughts about ourselves. Psychologically unhealthy people view themselves and the world around them in negative ways and are not able to function productively. The person who has a strong self-accepting attitude and feels adequate sees the world that way too. How might psychologically healthy people be described? Carl Rogers (1963) identified the characteristics of the fully functioning person as follows:

> We feel equal to others as persons.
> We have values we believe in strongly but are willing to modify
>   them if new evidence shows that we are in error.
> We don't spend large amounts of time worrying
>   about the future or agonizing over yesterday's mistakes.
> We feel confident about our ability to deal with problems.
> We resist the efforts of others to dominate and possess us.
> We accept the idea that we are capable of a wide range of emotions,
>   from being very loving to being very angry, from being very happy
>   to being very sad, from feeling great acceptance to feeling
>   deep resentment.
> We are able to retain confidence in our ability to deal with problems,
>   even though we have experienced setbacks.
> We are sensitive to the needs of others.
> We need not enhance ourselves at the
>   expense of others.
> We look for the best in others.

> We are capable of acting on our own best judgments, even if others disapprove of what we're doing (pp. 17-26).

All those characteristics on the above list are possibilities within the grasp of all human beings wishing to better themselves. Self-understanding and self-appreciation are not mystical goals beyond our reach. Our feelings about ourselves are learned responses; often bad feelings have to be unlearned and good feelings acquired. This is not easy, but it is possible. Taking stock of ourselves, doing a personal inventory, is an important way to begin.

So very many of us carry emotional scars which prevent us from living productively and creatively. It should be the goal of every human being to become a self-fulfilled person, to use all the potential that is inside. But, the individuals with deep emotional scars often become paralyzed and unable to move forward in their lives. They have negative self-concepts, feel unwanted, unloved, and incompetent. They see the world as a hostile place; they become combative, aggressive, and unfriendly. As a result, they also become frustrated, lonely, and sometimes antisocial. The woman who has been hurt by a man never wants to trust a man again. The man who has been rejected by a woman vows never to become involved with anyone emotionally again. The person whose ego has been wounded by an authority figure may develop problems with those who represent authority to him. Excessive protection against that original source of injury can make us extremely vulnerable. When we build an emotional wall as protection against one person, an event, or society, we cut ourselves off from other human beings and, tragically, from our real selves.

We need a certain amount of emotional toughness to protect us from real or imagined ego threats. Many of us have a thin-skinned ego. If only we can build up our self-esteem so that we will not feel threatened by every innocent remark or act. The healthy, strong ego does not feel itself threatened by acts of small consequence. We need to learn to grow thicker ego skins, but not so thick that it filters out all feeling. The cure for a weak ego is self-esteem. For the person with positive self-esteem, little slights are not threatening at all; they don't matter; they are simply ignored. Saying that we all need self-esteem, that we should learn to love and appreciate ourselves, is one thing. How to acquire self-esteem is the crucial question, and the best answer is to keep a journal. Self-esteem requires that we do something to be someone.

One of the most important steps in building self-esteem is letting go of old hurts. This involves a certain amount of forgiveness for others but, most importantly, for ourselves. Forgiveness, when it is real and genuine, is the instrument to help eliminate the scars of old emotional hurts. There is so much therapeutic value in forgiving, letting go, saying "past and done with." Carrying grudges causes festering wounds within us and often leads to widespread cancers within our spirits. Forgiveness is therapeutic; it lances, drains, and heals those festering parts as if there was nothing ever wrong.

What does it mean to forgive? To me, it means letting go of old grudges and negative feelings. Trotting out those old hurts, merely reliving and retelling, often embellishing them, serves no useful purpose; they become more deeply entrenched. It is another thing to work with those wounds, to step outside ourselves to look at them, to think about their infliction, to understand how it happened that we were wounded in the first place. Once we understand, we can accept, and then permit healing to take place.

It was journal writing that helped me to understand and practice forgiveness. It was important to open those old wounds, to explore fully the circumstances leading to their infliction. For a long time, I seemed to be afraid of looking at various pains in my early life. I think I was fearful of what I might find. As a result, I carried much within me that was unfinished. Once I looked fully and deeply and explored my feelings, I was able to say, "I'm finished with all that." I experienced a wonderful sense of feeling free and unburdened. The world looked so much more beautiful. I felt peaceful inside. Letting go of old musty baggage seems to have created space for fresh air and sunshine in my spirit.

Understanding leads to compassion. Compassion paves the way to forgiveness. When I became a teacher, I became aware of the importance of relating to children in a personal way. I learned how consuming that was and how easy it was to make mistakes. When I became a parent, I understood more fully how difficult it is to be totally responsible for another human being. I wanted the very best for my children and tried hard to help them become responsible, caring, and compassionate human beings. I made some mistakes, but I always loved them, and they knew that. I did the best I could for them.

I now feel compassion for my parents and marvel that they were able to rear six children during the Depression. I painfully remember how often they did without things in order to give to us. I remember how greedily I took, as if it were my due, often without saying a word of appreciation. They did the best they could for me, for all of us, in order that we could have lives better than theirs. My own childhood needs prevented me from seeing and appreciating all that, at the time. My parents are long dead, and I can't tell them about my insights and awareness. I deeply know now that they gave their best. Memories of their love and nurturance sustain me. I am increasingly able to focus upon that loving aspect of our relationship instead of the punishing one. They probably made peace with their parents in the same way. My children will probably remember and appreciate me more fully now that they are parents too.

I feel extremely fortunate to have lived in this era when we can openly express our feelings as well as our thoughts. My parents didn't have the knowledge available to them that I have; it was difficult for them to say "I love you." I don't remember my father ever saying those words. My mother said them to me as she was dying. How fortunate I am that I can say "I love you" to my children – and hear them respond in kind.

And so, I find that as I am more able to forgive others, I learn to forgive myself. Rather than dwelling upon the mistakes I've made, rather than beating myself over the head with self-condemnation, I've learned to appreciate and value myself. I've learned that the creative, self-appreciating person feels a need to give love as well as to receive it. I recall that I've always given a lot of love but have felt apologetic and embarrassed in the doing of it. I've let go of the compulsive need to have everyone love and approve of me. I have some close and cherished friends and, when I realize the extent of their caring, I feel blessed, doubly so that I can respond in my caring of them. I feel in charge of my life, responsible for my actions, and able to make choices leading to richer, fuller living. As I learn all these things, and as I do them, my self-esteem soars and the world is exquisitely beautiful. I'm reaching out more and receiving more. This time of my life is the happiest and best so far, and I'm anticipating all kinds of new and wonderful happenings.

I deliberately made this journey to search for self-esteem. In the process, a silent partner was spirituality. It seems to me that while pursuing self-esteem, spirituality ensued. Years ago, I was struck by the awesomeness of the human spirit when I studied Jane, and during my journey I've experienced the magnificence of the universe with all its living things and beings. Infinity comes to mind. We are all connected, and we were reminded of that by 9/11. Sorrows and betrayals have a way of touching our center, our souls, and offer opportunities for showing our compassion for ourselves and for others. I had a dream that through my self-esteem quest, I could make a difference in my own and in others' lives. I invite you to dream of attaining your heart's longing…

Strategies to Enhance Self-Esteem

THE FOLLOWING EXERCISES WERE DESIGNED to help you learn more about yourself. Through your journey, you may find misconceptions that influenced your self-image and self-esteem. As you gather your information, you will experience insights and awareness of the processes of living that shaped you. Work on forgiving old offenses, write about them in your journal, give away those old hurts and feelings. Laugh again in appreciation of those old joyful memories, relive the times which you felt well-nurtured and well-loved. Begin to explore roads not taken and look at old and new roads with fresh and adventuring eyes.

The present moment contains the seeds of what we can become tomorrow, next week, next year. It also contains the sum total of our past moments, everything we've felt, wondered, thought, and experienced during our lifetime. In a way, we are also the culmination of what our ancestors also experienced in their lifetime.

The questions and suggestions that follow for each chapter are intended to help you focus upon what's happening in your life, to help you begin journal writing. Find a quiet, comfortable place, reflect upon the questions and suggestions, and write whatever comes to you. Perhaps you will want to share these writings with another person, or perhaps you will want to read your responses "out loud" to yourself. I experience hearing my writing more powerfully by reading out loud rather than just reading it silently.

Chapter I — *I Began to Cry*

Go back as far as you can remember.
Think of the persons who gave you expressions of love and caring.
Who were the significant people in your life?
How do you know that the person cared for you?
How was the caring expressed?
Who are the nurturing/affirming people in your life now?

Chapter II — *Mirror, Mirror on the Wall*

1. Trust vs. Mistrust:

What do you remember about your early life: learning to walk, talk, etc.?
re there stories about this in the folklore of your family? What are your most vivid recollections? Do you have any traumatic memories of those early years? Are you basically a trusting or mistrusting person?

2. Autonomy vs. Doubt:

How were you punished as a child?
Do you remember feeling good or bad about yourself?
Are there any particular moments of anxiety or feeling criticized?
What are your first memories of feeling a personal sense of power?

3. Initiative vs. Guilt:

What is your first memory of feeling guilty?
When do you feel guilty now as an adult?
How can you be made to feel guilty?
Is this a device which can be used to manipulate and control you?
What was your fantasy life like in those early years?
How did you learn to cope with feelings of guilt?

4. Industry vs. Inferiority:

What do you remember of your early learning experiences?
What was reinforced?
Do you have any feelings of inferiority?
What are they?
How did you learn them?

5. Identity vs. Role Confusion:

Who were your adolescent heroes?
Do you recall any clues why they were heroes?
What kind of labels were pinned on you, such as in the yearbook?
Who were your friends?
Did you belong to a peer group?
How would you describe that group?
What kind of reputation did the group have?
Did you long to belong to another group?
Describe that group.
When did you first have a sense of who you were,
  and felt sense of your own identity?
Draw a picture of your self as an adolescent.
Draw a picture of yourself now.
   If you don't wish to draw, write a few paragraphs to paint a picture
   of yourself with words.

6. Intimacy vs. Isolation:

Going back as far as you can remember, make a list of the intimate relationships you've had.
Who are your friends now?
Describe an intimate relationship you are now experiencing.
   Is it symbiotic — good or bad?
How would you like it to be?
Who is your best friend?
What need does that best friend fulfill for you?
What qualities in your friends do you appreciate? — Not appreciate?

7. Generative vs. Stagnation:

Write a few paragraphs telling how you'd like to be when you're old.
Look for clues in what you write —
Do you want to play more?
Find a new career?
Do you have any plans for remaining productive?
What are they?
Who are the older people you admire?
What qualities do they have that you find particularly appealing?

8. Integrity vs. Despair:

What kind of integrity do you think you have?
Would you like to change that? How?
As you recall your life, what were the moments of most pain?
When did you feel best about yourself?
What are your most happy memories?
What could you do to recapture those moments?

Chapter III — *I Am My Own Worst Enemy*

In what kind of self-defeating behaviors do you engage?
How are you your own worst enemy?
What does being your own worst enemy do for you?
Have there been any self-defeating behaviors that you've ever been able to overcome?
When was that and how were you able to overcome that behavior?

Chapter IV — *I Am What I Own*

In the event of a fire, what is the one object you would be
   sure to take with you?
Why do you feel so strongly about this one object?
Make a list of your favorite material possessions.
What is it that you prize about these objects?
Take out your wallet.
Choose three things you value most of all the items in there.
Why did you select those items?
How do you feel when you are showing visitors your home?
When you hear the word possessions, do you think of material things
   or personal qualities?
Which of your personal qualities do you take the most pride in?
Do you own any status possessions?
What are they?

Chapter V — *It Is Ever Thus*

How do you react when someone says, "I love you"?
How do you treat the person who loves you?
Do you feel secure about that love?
   Or do you feel as if you might do something to lose it?
How do you feel about being very close to another?
What do you fear most about intimacy?
How do you express your love for another?
If you had to call someone for an emergency late at night,
   whom would you call? How important are friends to you?

Chapter VI — *By the Sweat of Thy Brow*

How did you decide upon your job?
How do you feel about your job: Is it satisfying? Boring? Exciting?
   What parts of it do you like the most?
   Dislike the most?
   Would you change your job if you could?
   Why?
   What would you like most to do if somehow your wish
      could be magically granted?
How could you go about making that happen?
How important is your job to you in comparison to other
   aspects of your life?
Describe your work environment.
What do you like about it?
What don't you like?

Is there anything you can do to make your work space:
    More comfortable?
    Livable?
    Reflective of you?

Chapter VII — *Getting Back to Basics*

Make a list of the great and not so great teachers you've experienced in your life.
    Why were those teachers great or not so great?
    From whom did you learn the most?
    When, in your educative process, did you feel best about yourself?
    Do you have any clues about how you learn?
    Write them down.

Chapter VIII — *As Ye Sow*

Make a list of the older people you've admired in your life.
What is it about them that you've admired?
How do you feel when someone asks you how old you are?
What is your greatest fear about growing old?
What in old age do you most look forward to?
What age would you like to be?
What would you have to do to live and work in ways
    that are satisfying and fulfilling for you?

AFTERWORD

The original manuscript of this book is like that distorted self-image to which I frequently referred. My opinions, lifetime learnings were there but buried in the quotations of the experts. I began by saying "Rogers indicates," "Freud thinks," "James says," and ended by saying, "I think so too." But then I began to say "I believe thus and so, and Rogers and others think so too!" A profound difference! And so, I went back this year and rewrote the entire manuscript. Even though there are many chapters of my evolving manuscript in the hands of family members, students, and teachers, this one feels more like me now.

I've learned that deep and true love of self, a true acceptance of self, leads to authentic self-esteem. We need not settle for the crumbs of life. We can feast at the banquet, if we so choose. When we are fully alive, saying a resounding YES! to the full human experience, potential riches can be realized. I invite you to feel and to be more like you.

Alice Zacharias Castner
Scottsdale, Arizona
January 2003

REFERENCES

Branden, N. (1994). *The Six Pillars of Self-Esteem*. NY: Ballantine Books.

California Task Force to Promote Self-Esteem and Personal and Social Responsibility (January 1990). *Toward A State of Esteem*. Chairperson, A. M. Mecca. Sacramento, CA: California State Department of Education, Office of State Printing.

Coopersmith, S. (1967). *The Antecedents of Self-Esteem*. San Francisco, CA: Freeman

Csikszentmihalyi, M. (2000). "Positive Psychology." *American Psychologist*. Vol. 55. No. 1. pp. 5-14.

Erickson, Erik (1968). *Identity, Youth and Crisis*. New York: W. W. Norton & Co.

Erickson, Erik (1963). *Childhood and Society*. 2nd ed. NY: W. W. Norton & Co.

Frank, Anne (1962). *Anne Frank, Diary of a Young Girl*. NY: Bantam Books, Inc. p. 40.

Heath, W. (1977). See: Jacobson, Robert (May 23, 1977).

Jacobsen, Robert (May 23, 1977). "Does High Academic Achievements Create Problems Later On?" *The Chronicle of Higher Education*.

Jaynes, Gregory (February 11, 1978). "Make It: 'Neither a little Snow...'" *The New York Times*, p. 35.

Jourard, Sidney (1964). *The Transparent Self*. Princeton, NJ: Van Nostrand Co. Inc.

Kanin, Garson (1978). *It Takes a Long Time to Become Young*. New York: Berkeley Books

Leboyer, Frederick (1975). *Birth Without Violence*. New York: Alfred Knopf.

Nin, Anais (1966, 1967, 1969, 1971, 1974, 1976). *The Diary*, Volumes I through VI. New York: Harcourt, Brace & World.

Prescott, Daniel (1957). *The Child in The Educative Process*. NY: McGraw Hill.

Presley, Elvis (February 6, 1978). "Trouble," as quoted by Corliss Richard in *New Times*, p. 65.

Progoff, Ira. (1975). *At A Journal Workshop*. New York: Dialogue House Library.

Rainer, Tristine. (1978). *The New Diary*. Los Angeles, CA: J. P. Tarcher, Inc.

Rogers, Carl (1981). *A Way of Being*. New York: Houghton Mifflin Co.

Rogers, Carl (Fall, 1980). "Growing Old or Older and Growing." *Journal of Humanistic Psychology*. Vol. 20. No. 4.

Rogers, Carl (1963). "The Concept of the Fully Functioning Person." *Psychotherapy: Theory, Research, and Practice*. pp. 17-26.

Rowan, Carl (May 5, 1977). Column: *New York Post*.

Sarton, May (1980). *Recovering: A Journal*. New York: W. W. Norton & Co.

Seligman, M. E. P. (2000). "Positive Psychology." *American Psychologist*. Vol. 55, No.1. pp. 5-14.

Slater, Lauren (2002, February 3). "The Trouble With Self-Esteem." *The New York Times Magazine*.

Talbot, Margaret (2002, February 24). "Mean Girls: And The New Movement to Tame Them." *The New York Times Magazine*.

Terkel, Studs (1974). *Working*. New York: Pantheon.

Ullman, Liv (1977). *Changing*. New York: Alfred Knopf.

www.ingramcontent.com/pod-product-compliance
Lightning Source LLC
Chambersburg PA
CBHW051803040426
42446CB00007B/500